THE WILL TO BE FREE

Books by Eric Williams

The Will to Be Free
The Tunnel
The Wooden Horse
The Escapers
Complete and Free
The Borders of Barbarism

The Will to Be Free

Great Escape Stories

Collected and Introduced by
ERIC WILLIAMS

281341

JOHNSON FREE PUBLIC LIBRARY
HACKENSACK, N. J.

THOMAS NELSON INC.
Nashville / New York

Introduction and Editorial Notes
copyright © 1958, 1970 by Eric Williams

All rights reserved under
International and Pan-American Conventions.
Published by Thomas Nelson Inc., Nashville, Tennessee

Second printing, May 1972

Library of Congress Catalog Card Number: 72-123112
ISBN 0-8407-6102-3
Manufactured in the United States of America

Acknowledgments

I am indebted to the following for their permission to use copyright material:

Messrs. Hodder & Stoughton Ltd. for the extract from *Evader* by T. D. G. Teare (THE EVADER)

Messrs. Ernest Benn Ltd. for the extract from *Rendez-vous 127: The Diary of Madame Brusselmans* MBE transcribed by Denis Hornsey DFC (THE HELPER)

Messrs. Dobson Books Ltd. for the extract from *Escape from Montluc* by André Devigny (CONDEMNED TO DEATH)

Messrs. Hollis & Carter Ltd. for the extract from *A Prisoner's Progress* by David James (THE "BULGARIAN" NAVAL OFFICER)

Messrs. William Heinemann Ltd. for the extract from *Horned Pigeon* by George Millar (CROSSING THE BORDER)

Messrs. William Collins Sons & Co. Ltd. for the extract from *Return Ticket* by Anthony Deane-Drummond (ESCAPE FROM HOSPITAL)

Messrs. Allan Wingate for the extract from *Dare to Be Free* by W. B. Thomas (THE LAND OF YOU-NEVER-KNOW)

Allan N. Medd Esq. for the extract from *The Long Walk Home* by Peter Medd, originally published by Messrs. John Lehmann Ltd. (JUMP FOR FREEDOM)

Messrs. Burton Publishing Company for the extract from *We Fought for Freedom* by Winton K. Sexton (THROUGH ENEMY LINES)

Messrs. Frederick Muller Ltd. for the extract from *The Edge of the Sword* by Captain Anthony Farrar-Hockley DSO, MC (ESCAPE IN KOREA)

Messrs. William Collins Sons & Co. Ltd. for the extract from *I Am Fifteen and I Do Not Want to Die* by Christine Arnothy (THROUGH THE IRON CURTAIN)

Contents

	Introduction: The Will to Be Free	11
1.	The Evader	21
2.	The Helper	34
3.	Condemned to Death	53
4.	The "Bulgarian" Naval Officer	70
5.	Crossing the Border	93
6.	Escape from Hospital	118
7.	The Land of You-Never-Know	134
8.	Jump for Freedom	154
9.	Through Enemy Lines	172
10.	Escape in Korea	186
11.	Through the Iron Curtain	209

THE WILL TO BE FREE

Introduction
The Will to Be Free

Since the end of the Second World War, many first-class escape books have been published. My problem in making this collection has been not to find exciting stories but to decide which to use. To shorten the list, I determined:

a. Each escaper must tell his own story, for only from firsthand accounts can the reader learn what it was truly like to be that man in that situation at that time; and
b. Each escaper must have been ultimately successful.

I admit I have broken rule (*b*). To stick to it slavishly I should have had to exclude the man who is perhaps the most invincible escaper in the book. I am confident that if the Korean War, in which he was taken prisoner, had lasted only a little longer, Captain Anthony Farrar-Hockley would somehow have got back to his own lines.

Not all these escapes are from actual imprisonment. Denys Teare, shot down over France, successfully evaded the Germans and is technically an "evader." Madame Brusselmans was never caught, but she spent four years dodging the dreaded Gestapo in Brussels. And the young Hungarian girl, Christine Arnothy, in breaking through the Iron Curtain, escaped not from a prison but from a whole country in captivity.

You will find here stories of escape by subterfuge, in disguise, by cutting barbed wire, climbing from windows, breaking through doors, jumping from trains—in fact, eleven escape stories showing eleven men and women escaping in eleven different ways. I chose my eleven and then discovered that I had not included a tunnel. It is an extraordinary truth that tunnels, the most popular means of getting out of a prison camp, were not often successful. Beneath Stalag-Luft III, the "escape-proof" camp built by the Germans especially to hold Allied aircrew, over one hundred tunnels were dug. Yet, although many prisoners got outside the camp by this means, only six tunnelers were lucky enough to get clean away. I think the main reasons why tunnels failed were:

1. The difficulty of disposing of the excavated earth;
2. The length of time taken to dig one makes the danger of discovery proportionately greater; and
3. The tunnels themselves were usually too big, involving too many people. When one broke, the Germans panicked at the thought of so many enemies at large and called out all police, troops, home guard, and Hitler Youth to search for the escapers. When I was a prisoner, I used to assess the chances of any tunnel in inverse proportion to the number of men who were engaged in its construction.

On the other hand, tunnels were popular because:

1. The escaper can choose his own time to leave and his departure can be unhurried and well prepared;
2. He can leave the camp ready dressed as a foreign worker, merchant seaman, or whomever he has decided to impersonate on his journey;

Introduction

3. He can take as much luggage as he can carry—which usually means food carefully hoarded from his share of the Red Cross parcels;
4. He can seal the exit after him and his absence will not be immediately noticed; and
5. A number of prisoners can escape at the same time.

To give my readers an idea of what tunneling was like, here is an extract from one of my own books, called *The Tunnel*, which describes my attempts to evade capture and my first escape attempt. Peter (myself) and John (Michael Codner, MC, with whom I eventually escaped from Stalag-Luft III through the *Wooden Horse* tunnel) have served their apprenticeship as "stooges," keeping cave for other escapers. They have been invited to dig.

"The scene in the central cookhouse reminded Peter of the setting for a modern ballet. The four boilers, like enormous witches' caldrons, stood side by side on an apron of concrete against the farthest wall. Beneath the end boiler, now dead, was the narrow entrance to the tunnel, open; and by its side lay the trapdoor made from concrete in a shallow wooden tray. In each of the side walls small high windows threw their spotlights onto the figures of the orderlies, who tended the boilers, and the early shift of tunnelers, who had just come to the surface. The tunnelers were dressed in woolen undervests and long pants, patched like harlequins, bright yellow from the puddled clay. On their heads they wore woolen caps or handkerchiefs knotted at the corners and, dancerlike, they wore no shoes.

"Tyson, already in his tunneling clothes, was waiting for them. 'Hurry up, chaps,' he said.

"Peter and John quickly took off their outer clothing and joined the new shift, who were waiting to go below. It was cold and they shivered as Tyson slid under the boiler and, after much grunting and straining, disappeared from view. Peter, following, found a hole in the floor about two feet square. There was a rough ladder fixed to the side of the shaft, at the bottom of which the flickering rays of a lamp showed Tyson's legs as he crawled out of sight. Presently his face appeared where his legs had been. 'Go easy down the ladder,' he said.

"At the bottom of the shaft was a square chamber about six feet by four in which a man crouched, working a crude concertina-like air pump made from a canvas kit bag. By his side the goon lamp cast its lurid glow across his sweating face as he swung to the rhythm of the creaking pump. The walls and ceilings of the chamber and the mouth of the tunnel which opened from it were of solid wood, bedboards jammed together side by side; but the floor was liquid clay.

"Tyson was crouching half in and half out of the tunnel. In his hands he had two smoking lamps, one of which he passed to Peter. 'Follow me!' He spoke in a whisper, as though he could be heard through twelve feet of solid earth.

"The tunnel, once they had left the chamber, was no longer lined with wood. The walls and ceiling dripped with water, which gathered in long puddles on the floor, and as he wriggled after Tyson into the blackness, Peter felt this water soak through his woolen vest and the cold grip him with its icy fingers.

"After they had crawled for about fifteen feet, the light in front stopped moving, and when Peter caught up with it he found Tyson crouching over a hole in the tunnel floor, about three feet from where the tunnel came to an abrupt end. 'It goes down another six feet,' he whispered. 'The real tunnel starts from the bottom of this shaft. The upper tunnel is only a dummy. We camouflage the trapdoor over this shaft whenever we leave it, and then if the goons discover the upper tunnel they'll think it ends here. They'll just fill in the top shaft and this bit of tunnel—and then when the flap's all over we can strike the lower tunnel from another shaft. That way we only lose the short upper tunnel, and save the lower one.' He chuckled and climbed down the second ladder into the lower gallery.

Introduction

"Peter, stifling his feeling of panic, followed. This was what he had wanted. He'd got the chance, and now he must go through with it.

"It seemed deep, deep down in the earth. Somehow the second shaft seemed a hundred times deeper that the first. It seemed completely beyond help from the surface. At intervals, where there had been a fall, patches of wooden shoring bulged ominously inward. He had to fight hard to force himself to carry on.

"He seemed to have been crawling for about half an hour before he again caught up with Tyson, who had reached the end of the tunnel. 'You work here,' Tyson told him. 'Here's a knife. Put the clay you dig out into this toboggan.' He showed Peter a rough wooden trough about eighteen inches long by twelve inches wide. 'When you pull the rope twice I'll haul it back to the lower shaft. I pass it up to the top tunnel, and John will send it back to the upper shaft in another toboggan. You see now why we need such a large team.'

"When Tyson had left him there was silence; more complete silence than Peter had ever known. It seemed as though the eighteen feet of soil above his head were pressing down, pressing inward. Then, in the silence, he heard the faint hiss of air pushed by the man at the pump through its lifeline of jam tins joined end to end. This metal pipe, coming along the upper tunnel, down the shaft and along the wall of the lower tunnel, was his connection with the outside world—that, and the rope which pulled the toboggan. He took the knife and began to hack away at the clay in front of him.

"An hour later Tyson called a halt. John took Peter's place at the head of the tunnel, while Peter pulled the clay back to the lower shaft. The rope, thinly plaited from the sisal string off the Red Cross parcels, cut deeply into his hands, and the strain of pulling the heavy toboggan through the thick sludge of the tunnel floor made his shoulders ache. He had blisters on the palms of his hands from the handle of the knife and, as he unloaded the clay into jam tins and passed them up to Tyson at the top of the shaft, he began to realize that there was more to tunneling than he had thought.

"At the end of the two-hour shift they came to the surface. Peter now knew why the earlier tunnelers had staggered as they crossed the kitchen floor. He had been sweating for the last two hours, and his woolen underclothes were wringing wet with sweat and moisture from the tunnel."

Only one of the escapers in this collection, André Devigny, would have been executed if he had sat back and twiddled his thumbs instead of trying to get away from his cell. Even a man held in safety and comparative comfort like David James, or wounded like W. B. Thomas, seized the first opportunity to escape. What is it that inspires weak and sometimes wounded men to jump into the darkness from a swiftly moving train, claw their way along the crumbling cornice of a building far above the ground, crawl under fences in the field of fire of enemy machine guns—risk death in cold blood as the men in these stories do? They could have remained in the security, companionship, and spartan comfort of the prison camp; yet they preferred the dangers and certain discomfort and loneliness of the apparently forlorn hope. These men were not fanatics. Their stories are told with humor, tolerance, and an eye to the other fellow's point of view. Why did they try to escape?

The answer lies, I think, in their independence of spirit. They had been caught: that was bad enough. They were going to do something about it themselves and not wait to be liberated. And they objected to being kicked around.

Escaping is essentially a lonely business, and an escaper must be able to dispense with companionship. His mental wholeness, or integrity, is more important than complete physical fitness.

He needs, then, independence of spirit and the ability to think and act alone. Above all, he needs luck.

In the Second World War there were prisoners who spent the whole term of their captivity, whether five years or one, in persistent attempts to escape. Many of them succeeded in getting out

Introduction

of their camps time and again, only to have the bad luck to meet an extra-suspicious ticket collector, a sharp-eyed youngster, or a too friendly waitress.

Not all the lucky escapers were lucky enough to survive the war. One of the greatest of all, the *Luftwaffe* fighter-pilot Franz von Werra, was afterward killed flying. Twice he had escaped from prison camps in England; the second time he nearly succeeded in stealing one of the latest Hurricanes from the Rolls-Royce testing field. The third time he was lucky as well as resourceful and courageous: he dived from the window of a moving train in Canada in midwinter and staggered to freedom in then-neutral United States across the icebound St. Lawrence River.

Von Werra escaped each time in enemy territory and knew that he could count on no help from the civilian population. In Europe, most Allied evaders and escaping prisoners made straight for one of the enemy-occupied countries and sought help from civilians. Unless the fugitive was unlucky enough to approach a quisling collaborating with the conquerors, he rarely asked help in vain. The men, women, and children of the occupied countries, and of Italy too, succored him because they valued the same ideals of liberty, respect for the individual, and human charity for which he was fighting.

The escaper would only lose his liberty if he was caught. The civilians who helped him risked interrogation, torture, incarceration under bestial conditions in concentration camps, and execution. After the war, the nations agreed that as civilians are nowadays inevitably involved in war, they should have the same rights as combatants.

The rights of combatants were agreed at the Geneva Convention of 1906. The principal clauses affecting a prisoner-of-war are:

1. He is the captive of the Government of the enemy country and not of the individual who has captured him. (In olden days a general could dispose of the prisoners taken by his

army. They were usually sold, kept as slaves, or exchanged for ransom.)
2. He must be protected by his captors from violence, insults, and public curiosity. (It had been the custom to march prisoners in chains through the streets to prove to the public that a victory had been won.)
3. When interrogated, he is obliged to reveal only his name, rank, and serial number; and no pressure may be brought to bear to force him to give any other information. (Torture was used by the Japanese in the Second World War against military prisoners, and by the Germans against captured members of the Resistance movements and British agents captured in civilian clothes.)
4. His permanent place of captivity must not be in a district which is unhealthy, nor in an area where he will be exposed to the fire of the fighting zone. He may be reasonably restrained but he must not be strictly confined except under absolute necessity. He must be properly housed and his dormitory accommodation and food must be the same as for depot troops of the captors' army. (In the Second World War the Japanese ignored all these requirements, and the Germans, although they usually obeyed the letter of the law, manacled some prisoners after the Canadian raid on Dieppe in 1942.)
5. He must be given freedom of religious worship.
6. He must be treated with due regard to his rank and age. If he is an officer he cannot be obliged to work, and, if an n.c.o., can be obliged to work only in a supervisory capacity. A working prisoner must not be made to work longer hours than a soldier of his captors' army and must be paid the same rate of wages. He cannot be required to do work which is directly concerned with the captors' war effort. (Again, the Japanese ignored these rules, and the Germans only adhered to them when convenient.)
7. He must be allowed to correspond with home and to

Introduction

receive parcels of food, clothing, and books. (Few prisoners of the Japanese received letters or parcels. In German prison camps the books were rigorously censored, and these and other gifts from home were often torn to pieces by the guards in their search for hidden maps and messages. In fairness to my German guards, I must admit that the parcels often contained things that no law-abiding prisoner would need!)

8. Attempts to escape shall be punished only by disciplinary action—usually a spell of solitary confinement. All forms of corporal punishment, confinement in cells not illuminated by daylight, and all other forms of cruelty whatsoever are prohibited as disciplinary punishment; nor may the prisoner be deprived of his rank.

Once the Geneva Convention had been ratified, escape from captivity became a game with set rules and forfeits for breaking them. Once a fighting man had been captured he gained certain rights and obligations and lost others. Before capture he could kill an enemy in uniform and, if subsequently captured, could not be punished for this. After capture he lost his status of "combatant" and became subject to the civil law of the enemy country. If during an escape attempt he killed a guard, he committed the civilian crime of murder and expected to pay the penalty.

On the other hand, since he had lost his combatant status by being captured, the escaping prisoner could disguise himself in civilian clothes without running the risk of execution as a spy—unless it could be proved he did spy during his escape. (Recaptured escapers often had difficulty in clearing themselves of a charge of espionage.)

It was a step in the right direction to agree to these humane rules. It would be real progress if the nations would abide by them. Individual men are not often, by themselves, brutal and sadistic. Bullies always lack courage. They like to have the excuse of "authority" behind them. The Japanese guards who beat helpless prisoners or chopped off their heads acted in the name of an all-powerful Emperor. The Gestapo men who beat up André Devigny, and those who shot in cold blood fifty recaptured prisoners after the big tunnel break from Stalag-Luft III, had the approval of the tyrannical Nazi régime. The young major who tortured Captain Anthony Farrar-Hockley in Korea had the backing of a system of government which declares that any brutality or injustice against any individual is good if it is done in the name of Communism. This is the difference between democracies and dictatorships. In a democracy the individual counts: the state is his servant. In a dictatorship the individual does not count: he is the servant of the state.

The Communists have added a new hazard to those faced in the past by the prisoner-of-war. They do not shrink from physical torture; they also attack a man's mind. They are not content to feed and clothe and keep him out of action; they must convert. They attempt by subtle means to destroy his self-respect so that they can replace it with their ideal of men as cogs in a mass machine.

Today individual freedom and integrity are threatened more than ever before. No one knows when he or she may have to meet a situation similar to the one which faced the heroes and the heroines of this book. Here are eleven vivid accounts by eleven individualists of the moment in their lives when they made their private choice and refused to accept defeat. Often single-handed, they licked the enemy. It is the unconquerable spirit of these men and women that wins wars. It is the spirit also that refuses in peacetime to bow to a dictator—the spirit that by fighting for individual freedom guarantees the freedom of peoples.

Each of these stories is an account of its author's escape from captivity, whether it be captivity in a prison or in a country. Each one is an escape from oppression, whether oppression by an alien enemy or by a government imposed by force. Each story is an adventure, because the greatest adventure of all is the adventure of taking one's life into one's own hands and depending on one's own resources.

1.

The Evader

The best way to escape is not to get caught. In the Second World War a great number of our airmen who were shot down over enemy territory managed to get back to England without being captured. These men who evaded capture were officially known as "evaders."

That they were successful was very often due not only to their own courage and resourcefulness but to the bravery of the civilian population among whom they fell. Denys Teare, bomb-aimer in a Lancaster, made his last raid on Germany on September 5, 1943. Although the aircraft was badly hit by flak over the target, the pilot managed to keep the machine in the air until they were over occupied France. Then . . .

. . . "Bail out! Bail out!" came the urgent order over the intercom, and I knew that a moment far more exciting and dangerous than anything I had yet experienced was close at hand. The crippled bomber was plunging down toward the inky blackness of enemy territory below.

At dusk on September 5, 1943, we had crossed the North Sea at twenty thousand feet, but after making our way through the reception thrown up by the coastal defenses, we had only three engines intact.

Although losing height, we reached our target, Mannheim, and found the Pathfinders had already dropped their green flares to indicate the target area. While we were making our run with bomb doors open, I could see the familiar pattern made by tons of explosives dropping all over the town. There were clusters of tiny white lights which kept appearing as the incendiaries landed, and among them the huge orange flashes made by the four-thousand-pound "cookies."

As the center of the blazing inferno slid below my bomb sight, I pressed the release button, and the slight upward lift of the aircraft told me that my own deadly load was on its way.

Closing the bomb doors, we altered course for home, but as fast as missiles descended from the five hundred or so aircraft in the darkness around us, so also were hundreds of shells coming up from the ground and bursting dangerously near. Being by now a mile below the rest of our compatriots, we soon began to receive far more than our share of hot shrapnel.

Suddenly the starboard engine, which had been pulling so well on its own, was hit, coughed, and died out. The situation was now rather grim; we plunged about the sky while Bob, the pilot, wrestled with the controls to stop the wounded monster from rolling on its back. We struggled gamely along through flak and fields of waving searchlights, losing height all the time. At first we thought that perhaps we would just reach the Channel; then one of the remaining two engines began to misfire.

A microphone switched on with a click and a voice came over the cracking intercom: "Whereabouts are we, Tommy?"

"About thirty miles from Luxembourg, I think," replied the navigator. Tommy was a born gambler, but I could tell by the tone of his voice that he did not like the heavy odds against him.

"Is everyone OK?" asked the pilot. Each man in turn switched on and answered—rear gunner, mid-upper gunner, wireless operator, engineer, navigator, and I. At least no one had been wounded, which was something to be thankful for.

"She won't maintain height," Bob continued. "We'll probably have to jump soon, chaps."

No one had the chance to reply, for just then the spluttering engine caught fire, the aircraft lurched dangerously and hurtled downward. With a last gallant effort Bob straightened her out once more, but she was still sinking. He pressed the button operating the fire extinguishers in the port side inner engine without effect; in a few seconds the whole wing would be ablaze.

We had practiced the "abandon aircraft" routine dozens of times on the ground, so when the order was given, each man knew exactly what to do. I had often wondered what my reactions would be on an occasion of extreme emergency such as this. As soon as Bob's words reached me, both hands started to work mechanically, first snatching off my flying helmet with its electrical leads and oxygen pipe attached, lest they foul the silken cords upon which my life was about to depend, then jumping to my feet astride the rubber pads I had been lying on behind the bomb sights, and then bending down to tug at the release handle. Up came the hatch itself, helped by the pressure outside; wind rushed into the aircraft and I felt maps swirling around my legs. My parachute was already clipped in position on my chest, so all that remained to do was dive head first through the square opening in the floor.

I felt the cold rush of night air as I somersaulted through the slipstream. On the first revolution I got a glimpse of the underside and tail of the plane silhouetted against the moon, but on the second the moon alone.

In the course of various lectures attended during training, I had learned the number of strands of wire used in the manufacture of a parachute rip cord, the strength of each strand, and the tests to which the completed object was subjected before coming into use. This instruction certainly increased the confidence of the pupil, but in my case I was left with the impression that the wire was made so strong in order to withstand the heavy tug required to release the parachute. In consequence, a few seconds after leaving the aircraft, I gave a terrific wrench on the chromium handle, knowing my life depended on it, and was horrified to feel it come away with no noticeable resistance whatsoever.

For a ghastly split second nothing happened and I continued to drop like a stone. Then something flashed past my face and a mighty jolt on the harness shook every bone in my body.

I had stopped falling and seemed to be standing still in midair. I gathered my senses together and began to take stock of my surroundings. I was alive; my parachute was above my head forming a big round dome lowering me to Mother Earth. I looked down past my dangling legs, saw that there was still a long way to drop, and felt very sick.

During the previous four hours I had heard the incessant roar of engines in my ears, but now there was a peaceful quietness, broken only by the sound of one single aircraft going away in the distance. Just then another thought flashed into my mind. Had the rest of the crew bailed out, or had I misunderstood the words spoken over the intercom? Perhaps the boys would be back in England at dawn; similar instances had happened in Bomber Command. A huge sheet of flame lit up the countryside a couple of miles away, then the sound reached me of a sickening crash and explosion. The silence was now unbroken, and I knew that old S for Sugar would definitely not see England in the morning.

Although I was slightly relieved to think I had not made a *faux pas*, I wondered if all seven of us were now drifting to earth, or whether anyone was dying in the wreckage below. I peered in all directions but saw nobody.

My descent probably lasted only two or three minutes, but during the time I hung in midair, it seemed very much longer. The ground below still looked black and threatening. Gradually the landscape became clearer, and in the moonlight I could see

The Evader

a wood directly beneath me and a small town at one side. The aircraft seemed to have crashed into a hillside. Quite suddenly everything became much clearer. I could see the little houses in the town, and the church, and then the trees seemed to rush toward me. I closed my eyes, covered my face with my arms, and curled up into a ball.

Crash! Branches rushed past me, then came another jerk on my harness as my parachute got caught in the treetops and I found myself still suspended in midair. After swinging about in all directions for several minutes, I finally wrapped my arms and legs tightly around nearby branches. Assuring myself that they were strong enough to take my weight, I gingerly released the buckle of the parachute harness and cautiously climbed down. With immense relief I felt my feet touch solid earth. One fist was clenched tightly, and, looking down, I saw that my shaking hand still gripped the rip-cord handle.

I did not know whether I was in Germany, Nazi-occupied France, or Luxembourg. Wherever I was, the procedure was the same. I tried to dislodge my parachute in order to bury it, together with my flying kit, but struggling in the pitch-darkness of the forest I found it a task far easier said than done. After wasting a quarter of an hour in a vain attempt to cut it away or shake it down, I abandoned the job. The few hours before daylight were too precious to be lost. Emptying the pockets, I regretfully threw my flying kit and Mae West in a heap on the ground. The trees were very dense, and there was a chance, unless a thorough search was made, that even the parachute might remain unseen indefinitely. Forcing my way in the darkness through the bushes, I kept in a straight line, aided by glimpses of the moon through the thick foliage, and eventually reached open fields.

In the clear moonlight I took stock of my possessions. My celluloid escape pack was still inside my battle dress, but when I opened it I found that the tube of condensed milk had split, turning the Horlicks tablets, miniature compasses, matches, and energy tablets into one sticky mess. Licking a compass clean,

I tried to read the tiny dial, but being unable to do so in the moonlight I stepped back into the wood in order to use the light from a match. Not one of the whole box would strike. I knew I would have to rely on the stars until the dawn.

I always carried a sheath knife on operational flights, and used it now to cut off the tops of my sheepskin flying boots, remove my brevet and sergeant's stripes. At the squadron I had been issued with a revolver, but had left it in the billet before taking off. My only other possessions were maps and Continental money in a waterproof packet which I would open in daylight.

From now onward, I was an evader.

I knew that my best direction lay to the southwest, and who knew—perhaps a few weeks' cross-country running would bring me to the Spanish border, and eventually to the British Embassy in Madrid. Setting off at jog-trot along the rough track by the edge of the trees, I pulled up suddenly as I heard a church clock strike one. Remembering the small town I had seen from above, I realized that it lay directly in my path. Leaving the track, I circled to the left across the field, avoiding the town.

Half an hour of hard running over potato drills, across fields, through hedges and barbed wire brought me to a wood even denser than the one I had left. Finding it impossible to make any headway, I retraced my steps and tried to get around to the other side of the town. Here again I found more dense woodland and also a kind of cliff, which appeared to form the edge of the town.

The streets were dark and deserted, so I cautiously made my way directly across the town. Reaching the first of the buildings, I was surprised to find them derelict; tiptoeing silently along, I found two streets of shattered houses with no windows, doors, or roofs. I learned later that this town had been almost completely destroyed during the First World War, and a new one erected at its side; of course, I had entered the ruined town first.

Leaving the scene of destruction behind me, I slid stealthily through the inhabited streets, keeping to the shadows. In what appeared to be the main street, I came across a route indicator, on

The Evader

which I read in the moonlight the distances to Metz, Strasbourg, and Nancy. I was thus able to establish my position fairly accurately, and was relieved to find I was actually over the border in occupied France.

While I was looking at the indicator, I heard a motor approaching and had just time to dive behind a pile of wood before it swung around the bend. Peeping out after it had passed, I got my first glimpse of enemy troops; the two uniformed occupants had probably been aroused to investigate the burning aircraft near by.

Gliding silently along the walls, I continued my journey, passing little cafés and shops with their various advertisements. Throughout the town I did not see a single window without shutters across it. The French people seemed to have a distinct dislike for fresh air, but this was perhaps an advantage to me, otherwise some sleepless person might have heard a slight footfall, seen a dark figure flitting from shadow to shadow, and given the alarm. The dogs knew something unusual was happening, however, and I could hear them howling from miles around.

Reaching open country once more, I heard the clock behind me strike three times, and realized that it would soon be daylight. I was still not far from the aircraft, and the German troops would be searching for her crew, so I went into a steady trot, which I hoped to keep up without tiring too quickly.

I plodded along for two hours, but my feet had become so sore that I went into a wood, crawled under a bush, and rested. The soles of my feet were like pieces of raw meat, for I had left off an extra pair of socks, thinking I might be too warm, and my feet had been slipping up and down in the big flying boots, causing blisters which had burst and re-formed. After bathing my feet in a stream, washing my hands and face, and filling my rubber water bag, I lay down to sleep.

When I awoke, it was about six o'clock and I felt very refreshed. It was a beautiful September morning, the sun was shining and the birds were singing. It reminded me of prewar camping days, and I would have thoroughly enjoyed a breakfast of bacon and eggs cooked over a wood fire.

My dreams stopped abruptly when I heard the sound of snapping twigs. Someone else was in the wood only a few yards away. I did not wait to see who it was, but I could vividly imagine a German soldier prodding his bayonet in the bushes, looking for the late occupants of the burned-out Lancaster. (I learned afterward that it was Bill Millburn, another member of our crew.) I squirmed along on my elbows for a hundred yards, then ran in a crouched position, keeping under cover as much as possible.

With the aid of my compass I kept in the same direction through the woods, seeing evidence of the First World War in the overgrown trenches I jumped over, which were still littered with rusty remains of barbed wire and steel helmets. A mile farther on, I came across some more recently laid barbed-wire entanglements and a notice board with large red printing on it in French and German. I could not make out what it meant, my knowledge of both languages being slight, and I thought it probably referred to the property being private, so I crawled under the wire. I went at a jog-trot among the undergrowth until I came to where the ground was dotted with holes. I then realized what the notice was—I was running over a German artillery range! Luckily no firing was taking place that morning, but when I reached the other side safely, I promised myself to walk around all red notices in future.

I was now into open country and, running along the hedges, headed in the direction of a smaller wood. Reaching this, I penetrated a few yards, then came upon a sheer drop of about fifty feet, covered densely with brambles and bushes. From where I stood I could see the River Meuse twisting its way through the fields. At the foot of the cliff ran a road which made an "S" bend, then crossed the river by a concrete bridge.

I realized that to continue in a straight line I would have to cross the bridge or swim the river. I could just faintly see two figures on the bridge, so I decided to descend the cliff and get as near as possible to see if they were guards or road workers.

The Evader

A narrow footpath zigzagged steeply downward through the bushes. I took this, but soon the steepness and loose shingle turned my cautious walk into an uncontrollable slide. Halfway down, on rounding a bush, I crashed right into a man trying to half carry, half push a bicycle up the pathway. I don't know who was more surprised, he or I.

I helped him to his feet and judged from his clothes that he was a woodcutter on his way to work. Letting my handkerchief fall to earth several times, I indicated that I had descended by parachute. He understood, looked anxiously in all directions, and was obviously scared lest anyone saw him talking to me. He glanced down once or twice, probably realizing he would perhaps be thrown down the rest of the cliff if I thought he would betray me.

He hurriedly went through his pockets and offered me some money, which I refused, showing him the French notes in my RAF emergency kit. I looked at his shoes, but they were not worth exchanging; they should have been in the dustbin long ago. So with a handshake and smile we separated.

Reaching the foot of the cliff, I left the bushes to walk along the road. My feet had become worse, and walking on the smooth roadway after the shingle gave me unimaginable relief. Hardly had I enjoyed this pleasure for ten yards when I heard the sound of motors approaching, and around the bend of the road came an army truck full of German soldiers, and across the bridge came a second one. In a flash I dived back into the bushes and lay there perfectly still, only a few feet from the road.

In each truck were about twenty fully armed men dressed in green uniform, half of them armed with rifles and bayonets and the other half with submachine guns. I realized that they were part of the search party turned out to look for the crew of the Lancaster.

When they had disappeared in the distance, I crept out and went toward the bridge to get a closer look at the two men. They were both in civilian clothes, so I walked past them with my hands in my pockets, whistling "Alouette" and trying to look unconcerned, as if I had lived there all my life. Even though my dress looked a bit queer, I could hardly be described as having a military appearance. I wore no hat, no brass buttons, no badges, and no chevrons. I needed a shave and a haircut and did not expect the French would recognize the color of my battle dress. However, these two men, as I knew later, had lived there all their lives and regarded me with suspicion while I was still a hundred yards away. Drawing level, I nodded my head and gave a slight grunt as if in greeting, but they just gaped at me in amazement. Walking right past them and over the bridge, I did not turn until I was two hundred yards on the other side. They were both peering in my direction; apparently I looked anything but a local inhabitant!

On either side of the road stretched potato and turnip fields, and instead of the hedges one sees in England, there grew apple and pear trees every fifty yards or so. They were laden with fruit, and, needless to say, I helped myself. I hoped to sight an isolated farm which I might approach without being seen, explain with signs and drawings who I was, and that the occupants would be patriotic and give me assistance.

After trudging along the dusty road for a couple of miles, I saw a car approaching. There was no cover at hand, so I ran quickly into the turnip field and knelt there pulling up weeds as if I were a farm worker. The vehicle passed by unheeding, so I continued on my way. For three more miles I walked wearily along without seeing a single house, but I was obliged to resort to pulling weeds on two other occasions, first for a cyclist, and next for a motorcyclist. On my right were a railway line and a canal, both gradually converging onto the road. Eventually I reached the point where they crossed; there I sat down and bathed my feet in the canal. It was here that I met Pierrot and M. Pierre, who were guarding the bridge.

In occupied France, every bridge of even the least importance was guarded, the main ones by German troops, those of lesser importance by local Frenchmen conscripted for the work. At

The Evader

certain times during the day and night, each bridge was visited by German patrols, and if they found a Frenchman absent or not alert, he was punished. Although these men were unarmed, they were expected to resist attempts by saboteurs or paratroops, and if the bridge was wrecked, they were held responsible. In some cases their families had been taken as hostages. The two men I had passed on the first bridge must have been on duty.

Pierrot was a very different person from the laborer I had met earlier in the morning. I will never forget the excitement in his dark eyes when he realized who I was. He danced around shaking my hand again and again, hardly believing that here was a real live *aviateur anglais*. He was crazy about airplanes; night after night he listened to the deep roar of our heavy bombers and in the daylight strained his eyes into the sky searching for the American Fortresses, usually flying so high that they were almost out of sight. He had wished time and time again that he could see a parachutist come down and help him to escape. And now before him stood an Englishman. At eight o'clock that morning he had been along to see the smoking ruins of my aircraft before mounting guard on the bridge.

His companion was a small, middle-aged man, very shabbily dressed, with an unlit cigarette drooping from his lips. He badly needed a shave, and the bottom row of his dirty, tobacco-stained teeth overlapped the top.

Alongside the bridge was a stone cabin, into which they motioned me. It was used as a guardroom-cum-sentry box, and in one corner a wood fire was burning, the smoke going out through a hole in the roof. The only furniture was a wooden bench, and on the floor was a straw-filled palliasse. An earnest discussion took place between the two men. There was obviously a difference of opinion, and it looked as though the elder wanted to give me some food and let me wander off, while Pierrot wished to take me to his home. At length a decision seemed to have been reached. Pierrot thrust two apples in my hand, then dashed off on his bicycle down the towpath.

When I was alone with M. Pierre, he seemed very uneasy in case anyone approached, but from his pocket he produced a piece of dark bread and a small slice of raw bacon. As he handed me the two together, his fingers trembled and the bacon fell onto the earth floor. Muttering curses, he picked it up, scraped it with his penknife and rebalanced it on the bread. This was my first taste of black bread, and although the bacon was now rather dirty, and smaller than a matchbox, I was hungry enough to be extremely grateful for it. From another pocket my host took out half a bottle of wine, from which he filled a small glass and handed it to me. It tasted rather sour, but I found it quite refreshing; twice I emptied the glass and twice M. Pierre offered me more, trying to tell me it was good stuff.

Unfolding my small escape maps and using signs, I asked M. Pierre to indicate where I was, pointing in the direction by which I had arrived. He repeated "St. Mihiel" several times, until I gathered that this was the name of the town through which I had passed in the darkness. I had found two handkerchiefs in my waterproof escape packet, one printed with the map of Germany on one side and northern France on the reverse side, the other one with maps of Italy and southern France. Searching through the German towns, my companion put his finger on Berlin, and, making whistling noises and indicating with his hands the dropping of bombs, looked questioningly into my face. I nodded my head and he shook my hand with great approval. I pointed out other German towns I had bombed, and managed to make him understand that I had never dropped a single bomb on any target in France. He grinned approval, spat on the floor, and babbled some incomprehensible phrase, which ended in the word "Hitler."

Fingering the map of Italy, he repeated his sign-language question. Pointing first to Turin and then Milan, with the accompanying sound effects, I gave my answer. He appeared slightly perturbed and said a lot more in French that I did not understand. Then he tried German, to which I shook my head and said,

"Nix," whereupon he changed to a third language which I believed was either Italian or Spanish, but still I could not understand him. At that moment, young Pierrot returned on his bicycle with a sack over his shoulder. He spoke to the older man, then turning to me and using the words *Mama, Papa, Babba,* gave me to understand that M. Pierre was an Italian, born in Turin, and that the rest of his family still lived there. Noticing my worried expression, M. Pierre indicated his attitude toward the war by spitting on the floor, banging his fist on the bench, and disgustedly muttering, *"Boche"* and *"C'est la guerre."* I learned later that he had never declared his true nationality when the Germans overran France, but continued to live as a Frenchman, proprietor of a little café in a village near by, where he lived with his wife and twenty-two-year-old daughter.

Opening the sack, Pierrot produced some civilian clothes and a note written in English which read: "Follow the boy, he will lead you to friends...."

... From that moment onward until France was liberated by the advancing Allied armies, Denys Teare was sheltered by French Resistance workers. At first, unable to speak the language and helpless in a strange land, he was passed on from one French family to another. Gradually, as his command of the language grew and he found his way to the more active center of Resistance, his life became more and more exciting, until toward the end he was a fully fledged member of a band of maquisards. Maquisards originally were men who took to the maquis, a thorny bush covering scrub country in wild parts of France. From this shelter they harassed the German invaders. Later the term maquis was used for all Resistance workers.

2.

The Helper

For the thousands of airmen who were shot down over enemy-occupied territory and the even greater number of our soldiers who had been overrun by the Blitzkrieg ("lightning war") of the advancing German armies in 1940, the only hope of returning to their own country was through the help of the civilian population. The penalty for giving such help was death.

In September, 1940, Mme. Anne Brusselmans, a Belgian mother of two young children, was visited in her Brussels flat by the local clergyman. "There are British soldiers hidden in the city," he told her. "Will you help?"

From that September morning until the liberation of Brussels by our troops four years later, Mme. Brusselmans and her family risked their lives every day to hide, feed, and finally to pass on to safety the charges who came to her flat for sanctuary. At first there were soldiers overrun by the Wehrmacht in its victorious advance; then there were RAF pilots shot down in dogfights over occupied territory, followed by increasing numbers of aircrew shot down on their way to and from targets far inside Germany;

The Helper

toward the end there were the Americans, floating down in their dozens from the daylight bombers which, hard pressed by German fighters, fought their way across the sky.

Mme. Brusselmans and her husband Julien became important links in the famous Comète Line, an escape organization that extended from Belgium across France, and over the Pyrenees to neutral Spain and Portugal. At the same time she assisted evaders, Mme. Brusselmans gathered information about German troops and military establishments to pass on to England.

The following extract from a diary this brave woman kept during these exciting years gives a vivid impression of the uncertainty and terror of her chosen way of fighting. . . .

. . . September 10

The other night I had to fetch in two Americans, Hank and Martin.

Hank hails from Chicago but is far from looking like a gangster. Mart comes from Ohio.

Martin still bears the marks of the heavy burns he sustained when he jumped out of his plane in full daylight. All his clothes were on fire. Everything he had on was burning except his parachute.

The two Americans landed near a river, which Hank helped Mart to cross by swimming beside him. He then took him to shelter among the bulrushes. Meanwhile, the Germans had seen the men come down and were searching the countryside for them, so they hid in this swamp for nine hours. At night they were helped out of their uncomfortable hiding place by members of the Belgian Underground, who, in a boat rowed by the young son of the local farmer, brought a doctor and a nurse with them to give Mart morphia and attend to his burns before taking them both off to the nearby farm.

After staying in the district until Martin's burns were healed, the two men came to Brussels. There was then the usual procedure first, at Mr. P's house, where it was decided that as it was late

Martin should stay the night, but that I would take Hank to stay at my house.

It was dark, and as we walked part of the way home we stumbled, for we couldn't see very much. The Brussels streets have cobbles that date back to the sixteenth century, or at least they feel as if they do. I know the way pretty well, as I have done this journey often in the heavy blackout, but Hank, poor man, I pitied him.

Hank, however, has given me some good advice. At least, he *says* it's good, or rather, good for the eyesight. "Eat as many raw carrots as you can," he says. "They are good for night vision."

Well, I'm not fond of carrots, either cooked or raw, but as they are about the only thing the Germans are leaving us, I shall have a go at eating them raw, as he advises. But, oh, for a nice juicy steak!

Halfway home we took a streetcar and it so happened that the two carriages were filled with Germans. I jumped in first and saw Hank hesitate, just for a second. Then he got on after me. We were the only civilians in this tram. Hank's face was most expressive.

There was no hesitation, however, when I went to get off. Hank jumped up double quick and followed me at once. He heaved a sigh of relief, and, as a matter of fact, so did I. If those Germans had only known what a bundle of medals they were missing.

The following day I took Hank downtown again to have his photo taken for his French identity card.

This journey passed off without incident, but on another one that night I really found myself in a tight corner. Two more Americans having arrived, I went off to fetch them in, and as we got on the streetcar, one of the men took out his cigarette case and offered cigarettes around.

Now, since the Germans have tumbled to a habit the Belgians have of burning soldiers' uniforms with their lighted cigarettes, smoking on streetcars is forbidden, although of course the Belgians soon found another way of annoying their oppressors. (Now they pour a few drops of acid on the uniforms instead, and then get off the streetcar.)

However, this was not the time to tell this story, so before the men had time to light up their cigarettes, I gave them the wink and we hastily got off the streetcar. They looked surprised to have to leave the car after so short a journey, but were even more surprised when I told them how nearly they had given themselves away. Of course, it is my fault, for I should have thought of warning them about this before. Funny how these small and quite innocent daily habits may lead us all to face a firing squad.

Arriving about half past nine at Mlle. C's house, I have a funny feeling, though I don't know why, that the house is not safe any more. So I ask the boys to stand by and watch. "If I flash my flashlight," I tell them, "everything is in order. But if I walk into the house without signaling, walk to the top of the street and wait for me there."

Then I walk up alone to the house and ring the bell. There is a short wait, then Mlle. C comes to the door and opens it. Everything was all right, after all.

We go in, and there they are all congregated, all laughing and joking. With those in there already, there are now twelve of them, and it is good to see them, and to hear them talk and make fun of their foreign civilian clothes. The Americans don't like the long-tailed shirts that men wear in Belgium; it's a lot of wasted material, they say. The British don't like the style of men's hats. As for the Canadians, they don't seem to care: all they long for is a good, strong drink. One tall American has wider interests—he wants to know if the use of peroxide is unknown in Belgium, for he has not seen a nice young blonde since he came here.

I returned home with the last streetcar to find Julien getting anxious. I suppose it is worse for those who are waiting at home than for those who are out on the road. But I could not resist staying with the boys to listen to all the latest news from England.

All are anxious to get back to take part in the big invasion, but after their description of the amount of planes and bombs they are accumulating on the other side of the Channel in preparation for this, I felt more like running away.

It's no use pretending otherwise; I do feel sometimes like nothing on earth. This continuous strain is getting me down. Yet I must keep on. I know that by now the Allies are counting on us. Again and again I remind myself that each man we send back is a man of experience, and that the mere fact that they do go back is good for the morale of those who, day after day, night after night, go out into the skies to face and meet death. And what a death! Burned alive or machine-gunned as they come down by parachute. Yes, we must keep on.

Word has come through to expect three more Americans. One is badly wounded, with a bullet in the leg. This happened ten days ago, and he cannot be moved from where he is because the Germans have encircled the village and are patrolling all the roads. The wounded man is hiding at a priest's house and as soon as all is clear will be brought into Brussels, where Mlle. C will take him in, for he must be sheltered where there are no children. Our doctor friend has been warned, for he will be needed. And so we are all standing by. Meanwhile, the wounded man is being nursed by a Belgian nurse who belongs to the Underground movement in the district where the man is hiding.

This week Julien took Hank to visit the bombed area. As Julien is an air-raid warden, he has a special pass, and arm band that enables him to enter the forbidden zone, so he got an extra arm band for Hank and off they went.

When they came back, Hank was speechless. It is one thing to be in a plane and drop bombs; it is quite another to be the target. Hank says he does not want to be in Belgium when the invasion starts (after seeing this). This sounds joyful to us. It looks as if we are going to have a tough time. Well, let it come. The sooner the better.

The Helper

Hank has left. I took him downtown at 8 P.M. He will stay one night with Mart and then leave for Paris. Thrilled at the idea of seeing "gay Paree"; he has made up his mind to buy some perfume for his wife—*Soir de Paris*, he wants.

In their place I have four more men to fetch. I shall get two in the morning and two in the afternoon. If these airmen keep coming in at this rate, we shall soon see them walk down the streets four abreast.

The Germans are getting to be a nuisance on these journeys. They have started the same little game as in 1914-1918—stopping the streetcars and searching civilians. For this the men must get off the streetcar and stand facing the walls with their hands up over their heads, while the Germans feel in their pockets, around their bodies, arms, and legs, and then check their identity papers. After this is done they are allowed to reenter the tram.

When the Germans decide to search the women, they take with them a German woman (a "Gray Mouse," as we call her) and she searches them and any children as well. It is useless to try to run away. Each patrol consists of twelve to sixteen men, two of whom stand in front of the streetcar, two at the back, and two on either side, while the rest do the searching. If one tries to run away, they shoot; and if arms or Underground papers are found, an army truck is sent for and all the passengers are taken away to the *Kommandantur* to be questioned.

Men aged between eighteen and fifty-five are made to go and work in Germany, unless they can prove they are working for a public concern, such as the police or the post office, or that they are employed by public undertakings like the gas and electricity associations or streetcars. In that case they have to produce special papers issued by the Germans and giving the name and address of employer and employee. It looks as if we shall badly need some of these papers very soon.

The wounded American has arrived and I have been to see him.

He comes from Virginia, so I call him "the Rebel." Poor fellow, he is not looking very well, although he seemed better on my next visit, after the doctor had extracted the bullet—or what we thought was a bullet—from his wound. (It turned out to be a piece of the plane.)

What we need now are bandages, iodine, and ether, and we can only get these things with a doctor's prescription. As it is a risky thing for a doctor to prescribe all this without being able to produce a patient in case of an inquiry, I went to see my neighbor the druggist to see what I could do on my own account.

"Mr. V," I said, "I need bandages fifteen centimeters wide, iodine and ether, cotton, and sterilized lint, and all this without a doctor's prescription."

He looked at me for a second.

"All right," he said, and a few moments later produced a neat little parcel.

"How much do I owe you?"

"Nothing."

I thanked him, and walked away.

"If you need any more, come back and see me," he called after me.

He had guessed, of course, why I needed these things, but as a very wise man asked me no questions and saved me telling stories.

Michou has been in with a letter from Hank, who says that he and Mart have had their journey postponed at the last minute. One of the guides has been arrested, and Hank is worried. He says members of another organization have been in to see them, and have promised to repatriate them at once, but he and Mart are suspicious of this and want me to take them away as quickly as possible.

I immediately went off to get Hank and Mart, but arrived too late. The woman sheltering them had let them go with these other people. I'm simply furious at this. It is the first time anything like this has happened to me. Who are these people? I wonder. We must find these two men; but why have they left? I had warned them not to leave with strangers. Really, they are worse than children.

Meanwhile, I have been to say good-bye to Stanley and his friends—two Americans—who are leaving tonight. I asked them to drink to our health on Christmas Eve and they promise they will do so.

Well, with all this journeying about, there is no getting out of it. We must steal or forge some of these *Werbestelle* papers, for with the Germans stopping and searching civilians at any time of the day or night, it is getting to be a risky thing to take these men out if they are not in possession of these documents.

The men are now leaving at the rate of ten a week. Not bad! I hope it keeps up, and it no doubt will, for I have received a letter from the south of Belgium saying that fifty more men are waiting their turn to come up. However, we are still busy evacuating men from the north of Belgium, who are arriving from the Holland area.

But with all these other men coming along, I am still preoccupied about Hank and Mart. There is no news of them, though their names and descriptions have been given to every Underground movement with which we are in contact.

There were two more men to get today, but I feel like taking a rest. I'm nervous. I don't know why, but I have a funny feeling again. I still feel that Mlle. C's house is not safe anymore. Too many people seem to know its address. However, no more men are to come to Brussels until all those we have here have left, and I must use this opportunity to look for Hank and Mart.

Hank and Mart have been found! Five weeks after they left. On learning the news, I insist they come back here, and that they must get priority on the departure list.

They have now arrived back in the flat.

I met them in the hall and said—"Well?"
They both lifted up their shoulders and answered—"Well?"
Then Hank spoke up.
"I was never so pleased to see a house as when I recognized this one."

At this I am afraid I lost my temper and was giving them both a piece of my mind at their stupidity, when Mart stopped me.

"Don't forget, Anne, we sweated this thing out."

He was right. It must have been no fun for them to be stranded in a strange house for five weeks on end with no hope of getting away. So we closed the subject by mutual consent.

It was worrying, all the same, for nobody ever found out what had gone wrong; the message that led to Hank and Mart being discovered had arrived by roundabout means, and the people who had taken them away remained discreetly under cover.

Just after Hank and Mart returned, the wife of the doctor who had to leave Belgium in 1942 came to see me. She had heard at last the message which her husband had promised to send her through the Belgian program on the BBC. Every morning at nine o'clock, personal messages are broadcast. This one told her that her husband is safe in England—the message which she has been awaiting for over a year now. She would like to let her husband know too that she is well, but personal messages are not allowed on our Underground transmitters unless they are very important ones. I thought the best way to help her would be for her to ask Hank and Mart to try to find the doctor when they get back to England. This she did, and they promised to do what they could to get a message to her husband.

Hank and Mart are leaving us. They must go at 6 a.m., which is an awkward hour for me, as the nuns living next door go to Mass at that time. I wonder what they would say if they saw me smuggling two men out of the house at this hour of the day! . . .

I have been out to buy overcoats for the two men. But Hank is so tall, and all I can find for him is an Austrian-type coat called a *Loden*. But I got a thick overcoat which fitted Mart quite well.

The Helper

Clothes and food are getting terribly scarce now, and can only be bought on the black market. Money is just as scarce, too, and I never see any come our way.

Mart and Hank started on their journey, with Hank still determined to buy his *Soir de Paris*.

I got up at half past four and made some coffee. Luckily, I have a big store of this, for the Americans prefer coffee to tea. Then I went to wake the two men and they started getting ready, putting on clean shirts and collars for the occasion. Mart seemed to have some difficulty with these, and was airing some of his strong Air Force language. After a quick breakfast, I tucked some sandwiches into their coat pockets and got them to repeat their Belgian names and supposed dates and places of birth, and made them show me what they must hand out if the Germans ask for their passport and what they must produce if the French ask if they are in possession of any foreign currency.

Then a last look over the balcony to see the nuns go off to church, and as soon as they have turned the corner, we all leave, having said all our good-byes before leaving the house.

We are the only three people in this important street and the sound of our footsteps seems to fill it.

"Well, here we are again," whispers Hank, "Anne and her two henchmen."

"Yes, Hank, and don't forget you owe me five francs for all the spots you made on my tablecloth," I whispered back.

(I make the children pay a franc for each spot they make on the cloth, just to make them careful, so naturally Hank and Mart had to do the same.)

And so we try to make light conversation, not that we feel in a joyful mood, but rather to hide our feelings. After all, the three of us are trying our best to escape from a ruthless enemy, with the odds against us.

At the station we are met by the guide and here, with a casual handshake and a knowing wink, they are gone. So, day after day, men not knowing a word of French go out to try their luck with fate, knowing full well the price they will pay if they fail.

Will this ever end? I wonder sometimes. Will next spring bring us the big event we all dread, yet are longing for? Time will tell, and meanwhile we are facing another winter and another war Christmas.

The children miss Hank. They gave him the name of Scaramouche, for he started to read a book of this title when he first came here and finished it before he left.

I shan't take in any more men for a few days, if possible, for we need a rest. I notice that every time the lift comes up, my small son Jacques runs to the sitting room to close the door if the men are in that room. He does not know these men are airmen, yet he seems to sense the danger when they are in the house. He also knows they are not to be seen by visitors.

To add to my feeling of disquiet, I have just read in *Le Soir* about the death by shooting of some of our friends.

This gives me an icy feeling down my back and I lie awake at night thinking of them.

What were their thoughts as they were being taken to the firing squad? Could they see the streets and the avenues they knew so well, on their way? Avenues and streets they were seeing for the last time. . . . Were they frightened, or was death a relief to them after their ill treatment?

These questions keep running through my mind, and I wonder if at their last ordeal they were thinking of their families, who were probably still asleep at home, but knowing that the last hour had come for those they loved.

If this happened to me, how would I take it? I wonder.

At this thought I shiver, and feel sure I would not be brave. I can visualize the whole scene. The gray dawn, the last cigarette, and the waiting around, perhaps, while the first prisoners are shot. The last few words with the priest, while the sound of the volleys being fired ring out. Then marching up to the execution post and, incredibly, that last word heard on this earth as the officer shouts, "Fire!"

The Helper

I see this scene over and over again in my mind until at last I cannot stand it any more and I get up. My eyes fall on a book, *The Pilgrim's Progress*, by John Bunyan. Opening it at random to glance through it, hardly knowing what it is I am doing but just, I suppose, to try to divert my thoughts into less gloomy channels, this is the first thing that I see: "Death is not welcome to nature, though by it we pass out of this world into glory."

I hope this is true. But, if the time comes, will the hope of it mean anything at all to me—and did it to them?

Last night I had a telephone call from Michou. Could I take two puppies at once? The mother is ill and one of the puppies has a bad paw. Do I mind? I answer, no, I don't mind and shall ask for a vet if it is at all necessary. Of course, I know what this means. Two men are to be transferred at once, for someone was arrested who was looking after them, and one man is wounded.

At 10 P.M. there is the conventional ring at the door—dot, dot, dot, bar. The V-sign in Morse code. I open the door and find Michou there with the two men. She tells me in French that she does not know what is wrong with these two, one of whom is English and the other American.

"They have not stopped laughing since I met them!"

The two men then greet me in French, and I answer them in the same language. They do not know I speak English.

Motioning them to the lift, I take them up in it and as we pass the second and third floors, the long, white-painted corridors leading to the company's offices can be seen. The two men stop laughing for a moment on seeing this, and then the tall American stoops down to the Englishman and mutters into his ear.

"Say, brother, this looks just like an asylum!"

"Yes, it will certainly sound like one, too, if you both don't stop all this laughing."

At my saying this, amazement spreads over their faces.

"Good heavens, are you English?" they ask in astonishment. This, however, is a question which is best left unanswered.

Bud, the American, and Lorne, the Englishman, soon made

themselves at home in the flat. Lorne has a bad foot and has to have it massaged. He also suffers with terrible pains in the head, for he had a bad fall when he landed. Bud is very helpful. He helps by looking after the central heating, getting the coal, and peeling the potatoes. I am glad of a little help, for every day I have to bake two loaves and every week three more loaves for friends who are in prison. This baking keeps me busy. After the war I shall never bake anymore.

The shop bread is too bad, the children would rather go hungry than eat it. We cannot get used to all this *ersatz* stuff. Luckily, Mrs. H sends me flour and keeps me provided with potatoes and ham. I don't know what I would do without her.

December, 1943
On December 15, we had a narrow shave from an unexpected source.

It was a lovely, clear day, and at 10 A.M. a Messerschmitt 109 came flying over the house; no doubt on a practice flight in the early-morning sunshine, I thought. But all of a sudden there was the sound of machine-gun fire, and I rushed out onto the terrace to see seven Allied fighters having a go at this Me 109. All the office clerks came rushing out too, from below, to watch the fight from the terrace. Just then, something prompted me to turn my head away to look back at my flat windows, and whom should I see there, still wearing their pajamas, and shouting and yelling at the top of their voices, but Bud and Lorne. I dashed in, pulled them both from the window, and then explained patiently why I had done so. I then went out once more to see the finish of the fight from the terrace. But no one had noticed the two men. Everyone was far too busy watching the Me 109 being brought down by the seven fighters, which flew away like white butterflies when they had finished what they had set out to do.

The day after this I went out with Michou and J to get six airmen.

Three days later, Michou comes in to see me late in the eve-

The Helper

ning and asks to use my telephone. Before we quite understand what is happening, she has asked for a long-distance call, and to speak to Jeanne. I could see that Julien was uneasy at this. He did not like the idea of a long-distance call from our house at nine o'clock at night. Then, as I listen to the conversation, I gather that Jeanne was arrested the day before, as were the two airmen staying with her.

Jeanne's uncle was arrested as well, but her aunt was still free, and it was she who was giving all these details on the telephone. Well, I thought, if the Germans have tapped their telephone line, we've had it. . . . As for Julien, he is furious, but it's no use just being angry about it, for the harm's done now; the main thing is: What are we going to do?

It's too late to move Bud and Lorne out of here now, and as Jeanne knows Michou's address and also Mlle. C's, I suggest that Michou move out with all her belongings at once. Bob—the Rebel staying at Mademoiselle's house—also has now got to be moved. He should have left some time ago, and would have but for a minor attack of appendicitis. As for us, Julien and I decide to stay up all night, and the two men stay on their beds fully dressed, all ready to clear out quickly if the Gestapo pay us an early-morning visit.

It is 2 A.M. We are still all on the alert, with our nerves tense at the least noise from the street, when we hear the sound of a car coming down the street. It stops, and then the doorbell rings. At this, we all jump up, the men making ready to get out of the kitchen window. Only Germans can circulate at this time of night. Julien goes to the inner door, opens it, and gets into the elevator, which he takes down to the hall below. We hear the elevator descending, but before he is halfway down, the doorbell rings again, five or six rings. There is no doubt now. These are Germans, and they are in a hurry.

The lift reaches the bottom floor. We hear the elevator gates open, and then there is a pause as Julien goes to the main door. He opens it, and immediately there is the sound of loud German voices, shouting out. "Why didn't you open up sooner?" a voice yells.

I can hear Julien arguing with the soldiers. The door closes, and there is the sound of footsteps in the hall downstairs.

They are Julien's, I think.

The elevator comes up. Julien is alone in it, as I had presumed.

We all sit down and heave a sigh of relief. There was a light showing through the window next door and the German police thought it was from our building—and that's all it was, Julien tells us.

Yet the German net is closing in, even if it missed us this time. Because of this, the journey to Liège that we planned has fallen through, so Bud and Lorne must wait. The escape route is blocked, and the Gestapo seems poised ready to strike.

Things are happening quickly. Mlle. C was arrested the day before yesterday. So, either the house was watched, or Jeanne had been forced to give the address. Well, for a long time now I had a feeling the place was not safe anymore.

Michou has been in. She has been followed, she says, but managed to lose her follower. I think it is high time for her to leave Belgium. The fact that the Gestapo is having her watched means they have their reasons for doing so. They don't waste their time following innocent people; not that I mean by this that we are criminals.

Meanwhile, I want a new contact to take her place, for the men keep on coming in at regular intervals, and it is now about time for Bud and Lorne to be on their way. They have been staying one month with us, and are getting restless, especially after the events of the last few days.

Before leaving with the two men for the station I had to buy a suit for Bud, and what a job it was. Why are these Americans so tall? It is so hard to find clothes to fit them. As for getting ten men like this one into a B-17, it looks to me that they must have to be folded in half before entering the plane. Yet they say they are very comfortable inside.

The Helper

The usual preparations begin as the time approaches for them to leave. First, I see that all their identity disks (or dog tags, as they call them) are securely in their clothes, for if they are caught they must be able to prove they are airmen trying to escape and are not spies. Lorne has a cigarette lighter which his mother gave him as a twenty-first birthday present. It has his name and address in it, so we have to find a safe place to hide it, for he won't leave it behind. The men are superstitious about such things—a feeling I know well.

Afterward, we walk downtown, for the Germans are intensifying their searches and it is easier to miss a search when walking than when in a streetcar.

It is 3:30 P.M. We have to walk slowly, for Lorne's foot is still a little painful. He is trying his best not to limp, however, so as not to attract attention.

On our way we have to pass in front of the building where the *Luftwaffe* question and condemn people for helping Allied airmen. Two German soldiers are mounting guard outside, and we pass right by them. They don't even look at us, and so much the better. "If I fly again, my first bomb will be for this place," Lorne whispers. Then we get to the station and it is good-bye once more. A discreet V-sign, with the first two fingers of the hand, and two more gallant men are on their way.

Before the men left, they helped me make a Christmas tree, but we are running out of decorations for it. However, the bombers drop a lot of aluminum strips to jam the German radar screen, and we are making do with this for decorating the tree.

This is our fourth war Christmas, and the children won't believe us now when we tell them it will be the last one. I have been going around the shops to see if I can find a few toys for Jacques. He is eight years old. Yvonne is twelve, and she has to understand it is impossible to give her Christmas presents. She is very reasonable about this and it makes it easier for us to tell her, but it squashes any hope she may have had. After visiting all the shops, all I could find were a few tin soldiers dressed in German uniforms, or German tanks, and German machine guns, all marked with the German Iron Cross and swastika. I just will not give such toys as these to my son to play with. I would rather see him disappointed once more. But I have made up my mind that when this war is ended, he and Yvonne will have all the toys they long for, even if it means I have to work until the end of my life to get them.

And so another Christmas Day comes and passes in wartime. I hope it is the last one.

I still need a new contact to take Michou's place. One young girl, about eighteen years old, who volunteered to go on a journey to Paris with two men to see how she would manage, was followed in Paris, so she won't do. Someone else has to be found.

Michou left on the fifth for the south. It is high time, for the Gestapo seems to be on her trail, but I must somehow get in touch with the rest of the helpers. I know there are about one hundred men waiting to be evacuated now. They are scattered about in different houses all over Belgium, waiting their turn to leave.

I have contacted Rio. He is the link with the northwest of Belgium, and he would like me to interrogate eight Americans from his sector. I have made arrangements to meet them in a school the day after tomorrow. I shall also have to have a photographer ready to have their photos taken, for it is getting dangerous to go downtown for this. Hitherto I have been to the Bon Marché and other big stores to have the men photographed, but always going to these shops with different men, I am afraid now of being recognized.

I was at the meeting place at 9:30 A.M. as arranged, but there was no Rio to be seen. I walked around the block of houses, looking in all the empty shop windows, then returned to the meeting place. Still no Rio.

At this, I decide to go on to the photographer's house. First,

The Helper

however, I inspect the house and the street. There is a man walking slowly down the road. Is he also watching? I wonder. I had better let him go by and see. No, he was waiting for his wife, who had gone into a shop. Reassured, I ring the bell of the first floor, though I know the photographer lives on the floor above that. A lady opens the door then, and I ask for Mrs. Jean, the photographer's wife.

"Mrs. J lives on the second floor," answers the lady.

Of course, I know this. However, I apologize, and ask if Mrs. J is in; does the lady know?

"Yes. I heard her walking about in the apartment just now."

Good, I think, with a sigh of relief. So far, nothing is wrong here. Then, going up to the second floor, I see Mrs. J there and tell her about the appointment with R and her husband.

R was arrested yesterday at midday in a café. No. this was all the news Mrs. J could give me.

I left, after telling her it would be a good thing for her husband to get a change of air, and went to our "postal box" near by—in this case a grocer's shop. For I want to know what has happened, and also to try to find the eight airmen. But as I am approaching the grocer's, I see the Gestapo coming out with a civilian whom at first I think to be the grocer. After waiting about for a few minutes I walk into the shop, however, and the grocer comes up to me with his face all bruised. I ask for two boxes of cleaning powder and, on paying for these and making sure there are no more Gestapo still in the house, give him the password and ask for news.

Bad news, is the answer.

"They are all arrested—five altogether—and I have just felt the weight of the Gestapo's fist," he says, adjusting his tie back into position nervously.

"One of the arrested men has been made to talk. They have just been in with him."

His eyes, as he was speaking, had a withdrawn, faraway look, and I did not press him for details. They generally turn your stomach, and I needed all my guts to face this new situation. For now I knew I was alone, on my own in Brussels, with no one to help me.

There was nothing I could do for this man, but I told him to clear out as quickly as possible. He is afraid, however, that if he does this, the Gestapo will take his wife and child as hostages, and it is difficult to find accommodations for three at such short notice....

... The grocer was arrested that same night. He was shot before the end of the year. Time and again, Mme. Brusselmans' fellow helpers were caught, tortured, and shot; and the escape organization was disorganized. Patiently and with the utmost courage she would piece it together again until the evaders were once more on their way to safety. She was a cool and careful planner and always managed to keep one jump ahead of her adversaries.

The diary was written at the time of the events it describes and, hidden under the floorboards, behind a loose brick, or in the garbage pail of the apartment, survived three searches by the Gestapo, who, although they suspected her, never found proof.

Madame Brusselmans was appointed a Member of the Order of the British Empire and awarded high Belgian and American decorations for her bravery. Above all, she earned the gratitude of one hundred and eighty airmen for whose safe return to England she was personally responsible.

3.

Condemned to Death

Not all resistance fighters were as lucky as Mme. Brusselmans. André Devigny was a member of the French Underground operating in Nice. On April 17, 1943, he was arrested by the Gestapo and taken to Montluc military prison in Lyons, where he was brutally beaten up, condemned to death, handcuffed, and placed in solitary confinement awaiting execution.

At first the small cell with its solid-oak door seemed to offer no opportunities for escape. Then, with a pin given to him by one of his fellow prisoners, Devigny learned how to pick the lock on his handcuffs so that he could take them off and put them on at will. This gave him freedom within the confines of his cell.

Next he noticed that although the door was constructed of thick oak boards, these were fastened together by tongues of softer wood. By grinding the handle of his iron spoon on the stone of the cell floor, the prisoner managed to make himself a joiner's chisel with which, after many days of patient work, he was able to remove first one, then several of the boards. This gave him access to the corridor outside, but he was still far from free. He knew that his cell was high up in the building and that his only escape route lay upward to the roof.

With infinite patience, Devigny began to twist himself ropes from strips torn from his bedding and reinforced with wire taken from his mattress. When this supply was exhausted he used his clothing—everything he could lay hands on. At last he had made sixty-five feet of rope.

Devigny's plan was to climb through a skylight in the ceiling of the corridor outside his cell, cross the roof of the building, and lower himself to an inner courtyard. From here, he would climb to the roof of another building, cross this, and throw his rope to the outer wall of the prison. To make this feat possible, he needed grappling irons on the end of the rope. These he made from the metal frame that surrounded the electric light in his cell.

Just as Devigny was ready to make his attempt, another prisoner, named Gimenez, was put in to share his cell. Devigny knew that should he escape and leave Gimenez behind in the cell, the boy, only eighteen years of age, would be shot for not giving the alarm. The only thing to do was to take him along....

... Gimenez took the boards from me one after the other and stacked them away. In the half-light we could just see the faint, barred outline of the gallery rails; it was too dark to make out the cell doors on the other side. I put out my head and listened. Only the creaking of beds as sleepers turned over, and occasionally a bucket scraping along the floor, broke the silence—that hostile silence against which we had to struggle for what seemed like a century.

For two long minutes I remained motionless. Then I pushed one arm out into the corridor, turned on one side, and crawled forward like a snake. I stood up cautiously. The light was on down below; but, as usual, its feeble rays were swallowed up in the vast gloom of the hall.

Gimenez passed me the light rope, which I at once took over

Condemned to Death

to the latrines. It was followed by the rest of our equipment. I went back to the cell door to help Gimenez. We both stood there for a moment, listening. All was still. Slowly we moved toward our starting point.

I tied one end of the light rope around my waist—the end, that is, which had no grappling iron attached to it. Three steps, and we were standing by the metal rod. The rope would pay out as I climbed; I left it coiled loosely on the ground. Gimenez braced himself against the wall and gave me a leg up. I stood on his shoulders, both hands gripping the rod, and tried to reach the edge of the skylight. I pulled myself up slowly, with all the strength I had. But it proved too much of an effort; I had to come down again.

The weeks of confinement I had undergone since my previous successful attempt must have sapped my strength more than I thought. We went back to the latrines to give me a few moments' rest. I inhaled deeply, waiting till I got my breath back before making a second attempt.

I had to get up there, whatever happened.

Jaws clenched, I began to climb. I got my feet from Gimenez's hands to his shoulders, and then to his head. My fingers gripped the metal rod convulsively. Somehow I went on, inch by inch; at last my fingers found the frame of the skylight, and I got my legs over the horizontal rod, which shook in its rings as my weight hung from it. I got around the ratchet supporting the skylight without touching it. I was sweating and panting like a man struggling out of quicksand, or a shipwrecked sailor clinging desperately to a reef. Eyes dilated, every muscle cracking, I gradually worked my way through the opening. Then I stopped for a minute to get my strength back. I had managed to preserve absolute silence from start to finish.

A few lights twinkled in the distance. The fresh night air cooled my damp face. It was very still. Slowly my breathing became normal again. Carefully I put out one hand onto the gritty surface of the flat roof, taking care to avoid touching the fragile glass in the skylight itself; this done, I hauled myself up a little farther and got my other hand into a similar position. With a final effort I completed the operation, and found myself standing upright on the roof, dazed by the clear splendor of the night sky. The silence drummed in my ears.

For a moment I remained motionless. Then I knelt down and slowly pulled up the rope. The shoes were dangling in their bundle at the end of it. I let it down again and brought up our coats. The third time I salvaged the big rope; it was a difficult job to squeeze it through the narrow opening.

Go slowly, I thought. Don't hurry. You've got plenty of time.

I unhooked the parcel and put it aside. Then I paid out the rope once more. We had agreed that Gimenez should tie it around his waist so that I could take up the slack and make his ascent easier. I waited a little, and then felt a gentle tug. I pulled steadily, hand over hand, taking care not to let the rope bear heavily on the metal edge of the skylight. We could not risk any noise. I heard the rods creaking under his weight; then, a moment later, two hands came up and got a grip on the sill. Slowly Gimenez's face and shoulders appeared.

I bent down and whispered, "Don't hurry. Take a rest."

He breathed in the fresh air, gulping and panting.

My mouth still close to his ear, I said: "Be careful how you pull yourself up. Don't put your hands on the glass."

He seemed as exhausted as I had been.

I untied the rope from my waist, and he followed suit. I coiled it up carefully, took a piece of string out of my pocket, and ran a bowline around the middle of the coil.

There we both stood, side by side, in absolute silence. It was hard to get used to this immense, seemingly limitless space all around. The glass penthouse (of which the skylight formed a part) stood out from the roof and vanished in darkness only a few feet away. I made out one or two small chimney cowls here and there. The courtyard and the perimeter were hidden from us by the parapet. We could walk upright without being seen.

I felt the shingle grit under my feet at the least move I made.

I took a coil of rope in each hand and picked them up with great care. Gimenez did the same with the shoes and coats. We stood there waiting for a train: it was five, perhaps even ten minutes coming.

Gimenez became impatient. I was just about to move when the sound of a locomotive reached us from the distance. It grew louder and louder; presently the train steamed past on the nearby track. We managed to get ten feet forward before it vanished into the distance again. The stretch of line that runs past Montluc joins the two main stations of Lyons. As a result it carries very heavy traffic, which had hardly slackened off even at this stage of the war.

We had nearly reached the middle of the roof now and found ourselves standing by the far end of the penthouse. A little farther on, a second penthouse appeared, which stretched away toward the other side of the roof. My eyes were beginning to get accustomed to the dark. I could see the large glass dome above the penthouse; that meant we were standing above the central well. I thought then for a moment of our friends below in their cells: some asleep, lost in wonderful dreams; others, who knew of our plan, awake, waiting in frightful suspense, ears straining for any suspicious noises.

We had advanced with extreme care, putting each foot down as lightly as possible, bent double, as if the weight of our apprehension and of the dangers we had to face was too heavy to be supported. Gimenez kept close behind me. I could hear his slow, regular breathing, and glimpse his dark silhouette against the night sky. We had to wait some time before another train came to our assistance. But this time it was a slow goods train. It enabled us to reach our objective—the side of the roof opposite the infirmary—in one quick move.

We put down our various packages. I turned back and whispered to Gimenez: "Lie down and wait for me here. Don't move."

"Where are you going?"

"To see what's happening."

Gimenez obediently dropped to his knees, and remained as motionless as the equipment stacked around him. I crept slowly around the corner of the roof, raised myself cautiously, and peered over the parapet. Below me I could see the stretch of the perimeter that flanked the Rue du Dauphiné. I lifted my head a little farther, and quickly drew it back again at the sight of a sentry. He was standing in one corner near the washhouse. I had known he would be there; yet in my present situation he scared me nearly out of my wits.

Of course he could not see me. I told myself not to be a fool.

I pressed my cheek against the rough concrete surface and slowly raised my head once more. Unfortunately, the wide shelf outside the parapet cut off my view of the part of the courtyard immediately below. As this was where we would have to climb down, it was essential to find a better observation post.

But before moving, I took another quick look at the soldier in the far corner. He seemed very wide awake. Soon a second sentry walked over to join him—probably the one who guarded the wooden barrack block on the other side. I saw the glowing tips of their cigarettes. The lamps in the courtyard gave off so weak a light that the men themselves were mere shadows against the surrounding gloom.

Occasionally a twinkling reflection from buckle or bayonet hinted at their movements. I knew that the best way of remaining unseen was to keep absolutely still. If I had to move, it must be done as slowly as possible, with long and frequent pauses. It took me some time to get back to Gimenez, tell him to stay put, climb over the parapet, and crawl along the outer catwalk till I was once more opposite the infirmary. A train passed by at exactly the right moment; I scrambled along as fast as I could to the corner of the wall. A loose piece of shingle, even a little sand going over the edge would have given me away. I would feel ahead with my hands, then slowly pull myself forward like a slug, breathing through my mouth.

In front of me, the perimeter was clearly visible. Beyond it, the tobacco factory and the buildings of the military court formed a broken outline against the horizon. Above them, the stars shone out in a moonless sky. After a little I could just make out the roof of the covered gallery over which we had to pass. Gradually our whole route became visible. I spotted a familiar landmark—the fanlight of my old cell—and then, on the left, the workshop and the women's quarters. Close by was the low wall between the infirmary and the courtyard. Soon, I thought, we should be climbing that wall. One room in the infirmary was still lighted; the light shone behind the wall in the direction of the covered gallery. I was, I realized, directly above Cell 45, where my first few weeks of detention had been spent.

I wriggled forward inch by inch, so as to reach the outer edge of the catwalk and get into a position from which I could observe the whole area of the courtyard. The two sentries were now out of sight around the corner of the block, smoking and chatting. I could see no one below me. The way was clear. My heart beat excitedly. A little farther and I would be certain. My face against the rough surface, I peered cautiously over the edge.

I was horrified at the gulf stretching down below me; I could not help feeling that my rope must be too short.

Nothing was stirring. I examined every danger point in turn—the shadowy corners by the washhouse and workshop, the women's quarters, the alley between the infirmary wall and the main block, the half-open doors leading from court to court, every conceivable hole or corner where a sentry might be lurking. Nothing. The cell windows were patterned on the façade like black squares in a crossword puzzle. Occasionally the sound of a cough drifted out from one of them. This, and the recurrent trains, alone broke the silence. Farther down, on the left, some of the windows seemed to be open. The stillness was almost tangible.

Still I scrutinized the courtyard with minute care. Suddenly a dark shape caught my eye, in a corner near the door of the main block. I stared closely at it. After a moment I realized it was a sentry, asleep on the steps. The weight of this alarming discovery filled me with a sudden vast depression. How on earth were we to get past him? How could we even be certain he was asleep? How—in the last resort—could we surprise him without being seen?

At this point the sentry sat up and lighted a cigarette. The flame from his lighter gave me a quick glimpse of his steel helmet and the submachine gun he carried. He got up, walked a little way in the direction of the infirmary, and then came back again.

Midnight struck.

It must have been the time when the guard was changed. The soldier passed directly beneath me, between the infirmary and the main block, and vanished in the direction of the guardhouse. Four or five minutes later his relief appeared. His footsteps crunched grimly over the cobbles.

A frightful inner conflict racked me as I studied his every movement, like a wild beast stalking its prey. We could not retreat. The way had to be cleared.

The sentry's beat took him away into the shadows at the far end of the court, then back to the main door, where the lamp shone for a moment on his helmet and the barrel of his submachine gun.

I watched him for almost an hour, memorizing the pattern of his movements. Then I raised myself on knees and elbows, climbed quietly over the parapet, and returned to Gimenez.

He was asleep. I woke him gently. "Time to move on," I said.

He got up without making any noise. I was busy untying the knot of the string lashed around the big rope.

"All set now," I whispered. "As soon as a train comes, we'll lower the rope."

I stood with one foot on the roof and the other on the catwalk, the low parapet between my legs. This way I could control the rope with both hands and pay it out without it touching the edge. I left Gimenez to control the coil and see that the rope was free from entanglements.

Condemned to Death

An eternity of time seemed to pass before a train came. At the first distant panting of the engine I began to lower away, slowly at first, then with increasing speed. When I felt the reinforced stretch near the end passing through my fingers I stopped, and lowered the rope onto the concrete. Then I hooked the grappling iron onto the inner side of the parapet. It seemed to hold firm enough. The rope stretched away into the darkness below us.

Gimenez would sling the parcels containing our shoes and coats around his neck, and follow me down when I gave him the signal. I knew that the moment I swung out from the roof into open space, the last irrevocable decision would have been taken. By so doing I would either clinch my victory or sign my own death warrant. While I remained on the roof it was still possible to return to my cell. Once I had begun the descent, there was no way back. Despite the cool night air, my face and shirt were soaked with sweat.

"Hold on to the grappling iron while I'm going down," I told Gimenez. I took hold of his hands and set them in position.

Then I crouched down on the outer ledge, facing him, ready to go down the rope at the first possible moment, and waited for a train to pass. Gimenez leaned over and hissed nervously in my ear, "There's someone down below!"

"Don't worry."

Then I looked at the sky and the stars and prayed that the rope would be strong enough, that the German sentry would not come around the corner at the wrong moment, that I would not make any accidental noise.

The waiting strained my nerves horribly. Once I began my descent, there would be no more hesitation, I knew; but, dear God, I thought, let that train come quickly, let me begin my descent into the abyss now, at once, before my strength fails me.

The stroke of one o'clock cut through the stillness like an ax.

Had an hour passed so quickly? The sentries' footsteps, echoing up to us with monotonous regularity, seemed to be counting out the seconds. There could not be so very many trains at this time of night.

Gimenez was showing signs of impatience. I told him to keep still. The words were hardly out of my mouth when a distant whistle broke the silence. Quickly it swelled in volume.

"This is it," I said.

I shuffled back toward the edge of the catwalk. Then, holding my breath, I slid myself over, gripping the rope between my knees, and holding the ledge with both hands to steady myself. At last I let go. The rope whirred upward under my feet, the wire binding tore at my hands. I went down as fast as I could, not even using my legs.

As soon as I touched the ground, I grabbed the parcel containing the second rope and doubled across the courtyard to the low wall. I released the rope, swung the grappling iron up, hauled myself over, and dropped down on the other side, behind the doorway, leaving the rope behind for Gimenez.

The train was fading away into the distance now, toward the station. The drumming of its wheels seemed to be echoed in my heaving chest. I opened my mouth and breathed deeply to ease the pressure on my lungs. Above me I saw the dark swinging line of rope, and the sharp outline of the roof against the sky.

I stood motionless, getting my breath back and accustoming my eyes to the darkness. The sentry's footsteps rang out behind the wall, scarcely six feet away. They passed on, only to return a moment later. I pressed both hands against my beating heart. When all was quiet again, I worked around to the doorway and flattened myself against it. I felt all my human reactions being swallowed up by pure animal instinct, the instinct for self-preservation that quickens the reflexes and gives one fresh reserves of strength.

It was my life or his.

As his footsteps approached, I tried to press myself into the wood against which my back was resting. Then, when I heard him change direction, I risked a quick glance out of my hiding place to see exactly where he was.

Condemned to Death

He did exactly the same thing twice, and still I waited.

I got a good grip on the ground with my heels; I could not afford to slip. The footsteps moved in my direction, grew louder. The sentry began to turn....

I sprang out of my recess like a panther, and got my hands around his throat in a deadly grip. With frantic violence I began to throttle him. I was no longer a man, but a wild animal. I squeezed and squeezed, with the terrible strength of desperation. My teeth were gritting against each other, my eyes bursting out of my head. I threw back my head to exert extra pressure, and felt my fingers bite deep into his neck. Already half strangled, the muscles of his throat torn and engorged, only held upright by my viselike grip, the sentry still feebly raised his arms as if to defend himself; but an instant later they fell back, inert. But this did not make me let go. For perhaps three minutes longer I maintained my pressure on his throat, as if afraid that one last cry, or even the death rattle, might give me away. Then, slowly, I loosened my bloodstained fingers, ready to close them again at the least movement; but the body remained slack and lifeless. I lowered it gently to the ground.

I stared down at the steel helmet which, fortunately perhaps, concealed the sentry's face; at the dark, hunched shape of the body itself, at the submachine gun, and the bayonet. I thought for a moment, then quickly drew the bayonet from its scabbard, gripped it by the hilt in both hands, and plunged it down with one straight, hard stroke into the sentry's back.

I raised my head, and saw that I was standing immediately below the window of Cell 45. Old memories fireworked up in my mind: hunger and thirst, the beatings I had suffered, the handcuffs, the condemned man in the next cell, Fränzel spitting in my face.

I went back to the doorway, near the infirmary, and whistled twice, very softly. A dark shape slid down the rope. It creaked under his weight. I went to meet him. Gimenez climbed the low wall, detached the light rope with its grappling iron, passed them down to me, and jumped. In his excitement, or nervousness, he had left our coats and shoes on the roof. At the time I said nothing about this. Clearly his long wait had depressed him; he was shivering all over. He gave a violent start when he saw the corpse stretched out near our feet.

I clapped him on the back. "You'll really have something to shiver about in a moment. Come on, quick."

Our troubles had only begun. We still had to cross the courtyard in order to reach the wall between it and the infirmary. Then there was the roof of the covered gallery to surmount, and, finally, the crossing of the perimeter walls.

I carried the rope and the fixed grappling iron; Gimenez had the loose one. We doubled across to the wall. It was essential for us to get up here as quickly as possible. The light left on in the infirmary was shining in our direction, and a guard could easily have spotted us from a first-floor window of the central block as we made our way toward the inner wall of the perimeter.

Gimenez gave me a leg up, and I managed to reach the top of the wall and hang on. But I was quite incapable by now of pulling myself up; all my strength had drained away. I came down again, wiped my forehead and regained my breath. If I had been alone I should in all probability have stuck at this point. As it was, I bent down against the wall in my turn, and Gimenez got up without any trouble. I undid the bundle of rope and passed him the end with the grappling iron attached. He fixed it securely. Then I tried again, with the rope to help me this time. Somehow I scrambled up, using hands, knees, and feet, thrusting and straining in one last desperate effort. Gimenez lay down flat on his belly to give himself more purchase, and managed to grasp me under the arms. Eventually I made it.

My heart was hammering against my ribs and my chest felt as if it were going to burst. My shirt clung damply to my body. But there was not a minute to lose. We coiled up the rope again and crawled along to the covered gallery. From here it was a short climb up the tiles to the ridge of the roof. We had to hurry because of that damned light; once we had got over the other side of the roof, we were in shadow again.

Unfortunately, I made a noise. Two tiles knocked against each other under the sliding pressure of my knee. Gimenez reproved me sharply.

"For God's sake, take care what you're doing!" he hissed.

"It wasn't my fault—"

"I haven't the least desire to be caught, even if you have!"

Since this was a sloping roof, we only needed to climb a little way down the far side to be completely hidden. If we stood upright we could easily see over the wall. Soon we were both crouching in position at the end of the covered gallery, our equipment beside us.

I was not acquainted with the exact details of the patrols in the perimeter. When I went out to be interrogated, I had observed a sentry box in each corner, but these were always unoccupied. Perhaps the guards used them at night, however; it was vital to find out. We already knew that one guard rode around and around the whole time on a bicycle; he passed us every two or three minutes, his pedals squeaking.

We listened carefully. Gimenez was just saying that the cyclist must be alone, when the sound of voices reached us. We had to think again.

Perhaps there was a sentry posted at each corner of the square, in the angle formed by the outer wall. If this turned out to be so, it would be extremely difficult to get across; nothing but complete darkness would give us a chance. That meant we must cut the electric cable, which ran about two feet below the top of the inner wall, on the perimeter side.

I half rose from my cramped position and took a quick look. The walls seemed much higher from here, and the lighting system enhanced this impression. A wave of despair swept over me. Surely we could never surmount this obstacle.

From the roof it had not looked very difficult. The yawning gulf had been hidden. But the perimeter was well lighted, and the sight of it—deep as hell and bright as daylight—almost crushed my exhausted determination.

I craned forward a little farther. The sentry box below, on our left, was empty. I ducked back quickly as the cyclist approached. He ground around the corner and started another circuit. A moment later I was enormously relieved to hear him talking to himself; it was this curious monologue we had intercepted a moment earlier. He was alone, after all.

Behind us rose the dark shape of the main block. We had come a long way since ten o'clock. Another six yards, and we were free. Yet what risks still remained to be run!

Little by little, determination flowed back into me. One more effort would do it. Don't look back, I thought. Keep your eyes in front of you till it's all over.

Bitter experience had taught me that overhastiness could be fatal; that every precipitate action was liable to bring disaster in its train. Gimenez was eager to get on and finish the operation, but I firmly held him back. I was as well aware as he was of the dangers that threatened us; I knew that every moment we delayed increased our risk of recapture. I thought of the open cell, the rope we had left hanging from the wall, the dead sentry in the courtyard, the possibility of his body being discovered by a patrol or his relief. Nevertheless, I spent more than a quarter of an hour watching that cyclist. Every four or five circuits he turned around and went the other way. We were well placed in our corner; he was busy taking the bend, and never looked up. We were additionally protected by the three shaded lights fixed on each wall. All their radiance was thrown down into the perimeter itself, leaving us in shadow. We could watch him without fear of discovery.

Three o'clock.

Gimenez was becoming desperate. At last I decided to move. Holding the end of the rope firmly in one hand, I coiled it across my left arm like a lasso. With the other hand I grasped the grappling iron. As soon as the sentry had pedaled past, I threw the line as hard as I could toward the opposite wall. The rope snaked up and out, and the grappling iron fell behind the parapet. I tugged very gently on it, trying to let it find a natural anchorage.

Apparently I had been successful; it held firm. A strand of barbed wire, which I had not previously noticed, rattled alarmingly as the rope jerked over it. After a little, however, it was pressed down to the level of the wall.

I gave one violent pull, but the rope did not budge. It had caught the first time. I breathed again.

"Give me the other hook," I muttered to Gimenez. I could feel him trembling.

The cyclist was coming around again now. I froze abruptly. For the first time he passed actually under the rope. When he had gone, I threaded the rope through the wire loop and pulled it as tight as we could. While Gimenez held it firm to prevent it from slipping, I knotted it tightly, and fixed the grappling iron in a crevice on the near side of the parapet. In my fear of running things too fine, I had actually overcalculated the amount of rope necessary; over six feet were left trailing loose on the roof. That thin line stretching across the perimeter looked hardly less fragile than the telephone wires that followed a similar route a few yards away.

I made several further tests when the cyclist was around the other side. I unanchored the grappling iron on our side, and then we both of us pulled on the rope as hard as we could to try out its strength.

If the truth must be told, I was horribly afraid that it would snap, and I would be left crippled in the perimeter. When I pulled on it with all my strength, I could feel it stretch. One last little effort and the whole thing would be over; but I had reached the absolute end of my courage, physical endurance, and willpower. All the time the cyclist continued to ride around beneath us.

Four o'clock struck.

In the distance, toward the station, the red lights on the railway line still shone out. But the first glimmer of dawn was already creeping up over the horizon, and the lights showed less bright every moment. We could wait no longer.

"Over you go, Gimenez. You're lighter than I am."
"No. You go first."
"It's your turn."
"I won't."
"Go on; it's up to you."
"No," he said desperately, "I can't do it."

The cyclist turned the corner again. I shook Gimenez desperately, my fingers itching to hit him.

"Are you going? Yes or no?"
"No," he cried, "no, *no!*"

"Shut up, for God's sake!" I said. I could not conquer his fear; I said no more. Still the German pedaled around his beat. Once he stopped almost directly beneath us, got off his machine, and urinated against the wall. It was at once a comic and terrifying sight. As time passed and the dawn approached, our chances of success grew steadily less. I knew it, yet I still hesitated. Gimenez shivered in silence.

Abruptly, as the sentry passed us yet again, I stooped forward, gripped the rope with both hands, swung out into space, and got my legs up into position. Hand over hand, my back hanging exposed above the void, I pulled myself across with desperate speed. I reached the far wall, got one arm over it, and scrambled up.

I had done it. I had escaped.

A delirious feeling of triumph swept over me. I forgot how exhausted I was; I almost forgot Gimenez, who was still waiting for the sentry to pass under him again before following me. I was oblivious to my thudding heart and hoarse breath; my knees might tremble, my face be dripping with sweat, my hands scored and bleeding, my throat choked, my head bursting, but I neither knew nor cared. All I was conscious of was the smell of life, the freedom I had won against such desperate odds. I uttered a quick and thankful prayer to God for bringing me through safely.

I moved along the top of the wall toward the courthouse

buildings, where it lost height considerably. I stopped just short of a small gateway. Workmen were going past in the street outside, and I waited a few moments before jumping down. This gave Gimenez time to catch up with me.

At five o'clock we were walking down the street in our socks and shirt sleeves—free men. . . .

. . . André Devigny had escaped from Montluc prison and in doing so escaped certain death. He made his way via Switzerland to Spain and from there to Algeria, where he trained as a Commando. With the Allied invasion of Europe he was back in France, fighting for her liberation.

Now Lieutenant Colonel Devigny is a professional soldier. He has been awarded many decorations, among them Commandeur de la Légion d'Honneur, Compagnon de la Libération, Croix de Guerre, Military Cross, Officier de l'Ordre de la Couronne Belge avec Palme, and Croix de Guerre Belge avec Palme.

4. The "Bulgarian" Naval Officer

Lieutenant David James, M.B.E., D.S.C., RNVR, was not a professional sailor. He was one of the many young men who on the outbreak of war dropped whatever they were doing to fight for their country in her hour of need. David James elected to do his fighting in motor gunboats.

On the night of February 28, 1943, his boat was sunk by the Germans in the North Sea, and after spending some time in the water, David James was picked up by the enemy and taken prisoner.

For the next year almost to the day (by which time he was a free man again in Sweden), David James thought of little else but getting home to fight again. The escape attempt I have included here is not his final successful break but an earlier effort which for sheer good spirits and humor alone ranks high in the annals of escape.

The scene is the naval internment camp of Marlag-und-Milag Nord near Bremen. Once weekly the prisoners are marched to a bathhouse outside the main wire of the camp for a hot shower.

The "Bulgarian" Naval Officer

David James has conceived the idea of climbing out through the window of the bathhouse while the other prisoners are undressing. He has decided to make his way to the Baltic coast in the hope of stowing away in a ship bound for neutral Sweden. To help him in his plans he consults Lieutenant Jackson, a member of the Escape Committee. . . .

. . . When it came to a character part for my journey, I naturally consulted the ingenious Jackson. He made the good point that the best possible guise in which to tour seaports was that of a seaman. As I possessed a naval uniform, this was easy. He suggested that I go as a Bulgarian naval officer, since Bulgaria was a monarchy, which would account for the royal crown on my buttons, and their Navy had only about three ships anyway, so I was unlikely to meet anyone who would know how they really dressed.

His final inspiration lay in the choice of my name. It was highly important that this should be easy to remember, because in the event of cross-examination it is the one thing over which one cannot afford to falter. Under the eagle eye of a Gestapo official it would be easy to forget a name like Vladimir Solokov, or Serge Filov. I therefore became Lt. Ivan Bagerov of the Royal Bulgarian Navy. (You may pronounce my name as you please. It is properly said like a well-known "term of endearment" used among sailors. I ought to know; after all, there are none like it in the Sofia Telephone Directory!)

This choice of character touches on another most important point of escape technique—it was essential to choose an *unusual* type. Any German official worth his pay would know the proper papers for German civilians, French "forced" workmen, and others that they saw every day. But a Bulgarian naval officer or an Irish groom would only come their way at most once or twice a year, so any papers, provided they were sufficiently imposing, would suffice.

Mine consisted of a Bulgarian naval identity card and an

open letter of introduction. The former was an approximate copy of our own naval cards. For a photograph we used the picture of a German E-boat hero, cut out of an illustrated paper. He did not look much like me, but it is a curious commentary on the gullibility of human nature that, provided there is a photo and it has a stamp on it, it is most rare for the police or customs of any country to look and see whether it resembles the bearer. In any case, to minimize this risk we put much of the stamp over the face.

There is a great art in writing bogus letters of introduction. They must be concise, yet contain a complete story, to save the escaper from answering too many questions. They must be vague enough to cover a wide range of possible activity, and they must be imposing without committing themselves to anything definite. In short, they must closely resemble answers to Parliamentary questions.

Jackson composed me a masterpiece. It said: "Lieutenant Bagerov is engaged in liaison duties of a technical nature which involve him in much travel. Since he speaks very little German, the usual benevolent assistance of all German officials is confidently solicited on his behalf."

Besides an official Bulgarian stamp—invented in the camp because we had no idea what the real one looked like—this letter was endorsed by three German stamps. One simply stated: "Heartily approved," and was countersigned by some mythical official of the German Foreign Office. Another, apparently from the Chief of Staff at Wilhelmshaven, said: "Permission to enter dock installations Nos. 9, 10, 11, 12, and 13 from 1st to 8th December." This was so that as soon as I arrived in Bremen I could imply that I had just come from the west and not from the east. The third read, "Identity checked by telephone from Berlin," and was signed by the Chief of Police at Cologne, whose name we had found in a German daily paper. This was to suggest that I had once previously been falsely arrested and had been released as soon as they discovered the mistake.

The "Bulgarian" Naval Officer 73

Most of the hard work for an escape lies in the preparations. Mine took almost three weeks and were very complete, for I was determined to enter as thoroughly into the character as I could. Bulgarians cannot pronounce the "eu" sound in words like *deutsch*. Instead of saying it like the "oy" in boy, they pronounce it like the "ye" in bye. To acquire this habit I used to read out aloud the editorials from the *DAZ and Das Reich "à la bulgare."* The Bulgar also uses Russian characters in writing, so in order to be able to make a signature similar to that on my identity card I had to spend ten minutes every day practicing it.

I resolved to take a small case with food and a change of clothing. Every article of wear was marked with my new name, and I scraped the name of the maker off my soap and put a Bulgarian hieroglyphic on instead. There were two Greek officers in the camp, and, as the nearest possible thing, I asked them for their tailors' tabs and sewed them in my uniform and cap. By the time I had finished, there was nothing on my person or in my case to suggest that I was English. I even carried in my pocket a series of "love letters" written in off-Russian by Jackson in a very feminine hand.

It is most desirable to have something about one to distract the attention of any searcher from his job. I had the perfect thing to hand. One of my interests has always been the ballet, and when I was captured, a friend very kindly sent me some very fine half-plate photographs of the Sadler's Wells. One of these was a lovely full-face portrait of Margot Fonteyn in ballroom dress, from the ballet *Apparitions*. With her dark coloring and exotic beauty, this was just what I wanted. A short inscription in Russian was added, and she became "my fiancée at the German Legation ball in Sofia." The only time my case was ever searched, this picture occasioned far more interest than all the rest of the contents put together.

A number of articles I sewed into my clothing. There was a pocket in my trouser leg in which I carried a recent letter from home to prove my identity to any neutrals or other potential helpers. My tally [identity disk] was sewn under one armpit and a spare sum of money under the other.

The only alteration, or, rather, addition to my uniform was a five-letter flash—gold on a blue ground—on my left shoulder, standing for the initial letters of *"Kralov Bulgrski Voyenno-Mrskoi Flot,"* or Royal Bulgarian Navy.

And now, just when I thought I had everything prepared, I found a weakness in my scheme. One day a group of prisoners was taken by train into Bremen to see the oculist. This meant that my uniform would be recognized on the local line. I was therefore forced to adopt an entirely different character part for the first part of the journey.

I decided that I would travel into Bremen as a Danish electrician. My story would be that my nerves had been severely shattered in a recent raid, I had been spending a week in the country to recuperate, and was on my way back for medical survey. For papers I had a temporary identity card (*Vorläufiger Ausweis*) and a note from the hospital (written, in fact, by Johnny Pryor, the escape representative), telling me to report there on the afternoon of December 8.

For my quick change at the bathhouse I meant to go up in uniform with a greatcoat on, and with gray flannel trousers over my blues, but rolled up above the knee so that they shouldn't show. I had a checked scarf well tucked down underneath my coat collar and a cloth cap made out of a blanket in one pocket. My shoulder straps and belt were on hooks, so that they were readily detachable. The front buttons of my coat I had covered with black silk, so that at a casual glance they looked like civilian buttons. To change then, all I had to do was rip off the belt and shoulder straps, roll down my trousers, pull up my scarf, and don the cap. I practiced this operation a number of times, till ultimately it took me less than thirty seconds.

All was now set. My final plan was to go up with the bath party, change, and drop out of the window, then walk down the road for about half a mile, to where there was a small coppice. Here I proposed to kill half an hour putting on a few bandages and otherwise altering my appearance before walking to the station just in time to catch the 11:50 train. This train was scheduled to arrive at Bremen at 1:20 p.m. and to start on its return journey ten minutes later. There would be such a crowd on arrival that I hoped to pass unobserved into the station lavatory. There I would discard my civilian clothes, and, once the train had left, emerge onto an empty platform as a Bulgarian. From then on my journey up to the Baltic ports should be fairly easy.

So many times had I rehearsed this scheme in my mind that I could almost believe I had done it. Only the play *Ten Minute Alibi*, performed in the camp a short time before, depressed me. For that showed only too well what a discrepancy there can be between the well-oiled plan of the imagination and its counterpart of obstinate fact.

The strange thing is that this one did run almost perfectly to schedule.

Thursday, December 8, dawned cold and foggy. I awoke early and went to Mass; for I wanted to start with the blessing of God. After breakfast there was the usual last-minute rush to complete the preparations. The night before, I had been sure that all was ready, but a whole series of last-minute details cropped up.

I had a small team of assistants for the job. There were Jackson and Bill Tillie to keep the guards talking and to persuade them that nobody was away should they find themselves one short. Johnny Pryor and Roddy were to come as close support. Their job was to stand in the doorways leading in from the two changing-rooms and to start taking their greatcoats off as soon as the guards entered. This would act as a signal to let me know there were no guards left outside the building, and prevent them from seeing me as I got through the window.

But long before we started out, there was plenty for them to do. It must have taken six men to get me dressed and ready. Where was I going to keep my Bulgarian papers while posing as a Dane? It would never do to get them muddled up. Somebody suggested strapping them to the inside of my thigh, and rushed off to the sick bay for sticking plaster. I had better take needles and thread, but at the last minute could not find my "hussif" . . . and so on. But at last my bag was packed. It had proved rather a squash getting all my food in, and my naval cap had to be jammed on top at the last moment.

The first bath party came back and reported that the guards were being slacker than usual. The second party were now up having their shower, so just before 10:45 we began to form up in threes at the main gate. With Jackson and Johnny Pryor, I was in the second row. Roddy, who was looking more villainous than ever and was thoroughly enjoying himself, had volunteered to carry up my case and was a few rows farther back.

As the second party came into view, streaming out from the bathhouse, I was seized with a spasm of acute regret. The day was grim and misty, and there was a nice fire burning in our room. I was happy and busy in the camp. Why was I such a fool as to leave when the war was bound to end in a few months anyway? Why risk being shot for a hundred-to-one chance of freedom?

The second party came through the gate, and I got a thumbs-up from Commander Beale, who had gone to see for himself how the guards were behaving. There was a horrid feeling in the pit of my stomach when we began to move forward. I was committed now, and there was no way out, but how I wished that the *Kommandant* would cancel the last bath, or the water would run cold, or something else would occur to get me out of this foolish venture!

I heard laughter behind me and the column came to a halt. Looking back, I saw Roddy, surrounded by three guards, stooping down. Hell! The lock on the case had burst and my gear was spread all over the road. I could see a packet of sandwiches sitting disconsolately by the edge of a puddle. How could even

The "Bulgarian" Naval Officer

German guards fail to regard this as an unusual aid to bathing? But Roddy stuffed everything back again and closed the case, just as though he always took chocolate and cheese to his bath.

We moved off again, this time everyone straggling according to plan, so as to increase the delay in getting into the changing rooms to give me more time to change. Roddy sidled up alongside and whispered to me that in repacking my case he had put my cap in the other way around. The badge now faced the hinge and not the outside. I thanked him perfunctorily. I did not then know that had it not been for this, I would certainly never have got away. . . .

As I went into the changing-room I was already rolling down my trousers. Thirty seconds later I was a civilian and passed through into the bathroom. Roddy was standing by the far bathroom door. As soon as he started to take his coat off, I knew that the guards were inside. Looking around, I found that Johnny Pryor was doing the same. With a quite unnecessary clatter, which would have given the game away to anyone less sleepy than our guards, I climbed through the window and dropped out. As I walked past the bathhouse I heard the sound of footsteps running on the concrete. Was it one of the guards? Was he going to shoot? I didn't dare look back, but continued to shuffle off as speedily as was consistent with innocence. Behind me I heard a door slam, and then all was quiet. . . .

At once a new danger loomed ahead. Up the hill from the camp there was coming Joseph, a German who knew me better than anyone. He was riding a bicycle, his head lowered, after the manner of one pedaling up an incline. I had to turn right to gain the main road, but Joseph and I were almost equidistant from the turning. Could I get there first, and would he or would he not look up and spot me? I could not afford to run, but I reached the turn with Joseph still ten feet away. He never gave me a glance.

Despite fog and drizzle, the main road, which was absolutely straight and without cover for over a mile, was unduly populous.

Two Germans I knew by sight passed me without giving signs of recognition. There was, in any case, nothing I could do about it except to trudge on, looking as innocent as I could. Apart from the worry, I was beginning to enjoy myself. All the anticipations and regrets had vanished the moment I dropped out of the window and saw freedom stretching ahead down that long road.

I was in this happy frame of mind when a tall figure in field gray, passing on a bicycle, gave me a dirty look and called on me to stop.

This first investigation was a great test, and I could hardly control my nerves.

"Who are you?"

"Paul Hanson—a Dane."

"Where are your papers?"

"Here" said I, giving him my temporary pass, which was of imitation typewriting, in pencil.

"Where were you born?"

"Aarhus." (Thank goodness I'd memorized all my details.)

"When were you born?"

"Fifth of October." (My mother's birthday.)

"Is that your photograph?" said he, pointing at the small picture of a fair-haired man in golfing jacket, stuck on my pass.

With a nasty feeling in the pit of my stomach, I realized that I had grown a moustache, but had failed to add one to this photograph. Furthermore, he wore spectacles, and I had forgotten to take mine with me. Ignoring those discrepancies, I said, "Of course," in as pained a tone as I could. To my surprise he handed me back my pass without further comment.

"What are you doing here?"

"I am an employee of AEG, Bremen. I was wounded in the raid on the twenty-third of November and have been sent out for a week to rest my nerves. I'm now returning to the hospital for survey." (This nerve story might discount any suspicion caused by my ill-concealed agitation.)

"Where have you been staying?"

"With the parson at Kirchtimke." (There ought to be one at a place with a name like that.)

"Which one? What was he called?"

"I don't know his name. Everyone called him '*Pfarrer*' (Pastor). The chap with the gray hair, I mean." (A fairly good bet that there wouldn't be any young ones left.)

"H'm. Where did he live?"

"In the little house by the church." (That is the usual North German layout.)

"Let's see inside that case of yours."

Now I was in for it. Propping it on the seat of his bike, I opened the wretched thing up.

"H'm. Shirt, bread, cigarettes, sweater. What's in that paper parcel there?" He pointed to my chocolate wrapped in an old newspaper.

"More bread."

"What's this?" he asked, lifting the back of my cap. (Thank goodness Roddy had turned it around.)

"My working cap."

There was an ugly pause. He clearly had a residue of doubt lingering in his mind, which can hardly be wondered at, since he was the local policeman and we were still within half a mile of the camp. If he took me into custody I should be finished, for I could hardly survive a more searching cross-examination.

I produced my last trump card, Johnny Pryor's letter, purporting to be from the medical superintendent at Bremen Hospital, directing me to report back that afternoon. I gave it to him and the scales tipped in my favor. Pointing down, he said, "Some of your cigarettes have fallen on the ground," mounted his bicycle, and was off. I stood in the middle of the road with my mouth open, clutching my case in both arms like a baby.

Continuing along the road, I dived into a wood, bandaged my head, and shaved off half my eyebrows. The fog was thicker, and I emerged on the road again just behind a girl carrying a small suitcase. Evidently she was catching the train too, so I followed her to the station. It was later than I thought, and we had to run the last few hundred yards.

Buying the ticket presented no difficulty, and I climbed into a non-smoker full of typical German housewives. No one paid any attention to the sad-looking young man with a bandaged head, who sat by himself in a corner. The fat woman opposite was soon fast asleep. It was just as well. Halfway to Bremen I looked down and saw that the silk cover had fallen off one of my buttons. Nobody appeared to have noticed, so I hid it under my cap and then cut it off.

It was 1:15 when we arrived in Bremen, and there was a crowd on the platform waiting to go back to Tarmstedt on the 1:30 train. Together with several others, I went into the public lavatory. It was primitive and the light was shocking, but there was a bolt on the door. With great excitement, for the situation was becoming increasingly Edgar-Wallace-like, I removed my civilian trousers and stuffed the cap behind some pipes. Off with button covers and on with the greatcoat belt. I then blacked my moustache and darkened my eyes, as I had been taught by the theatrical makeup experts. Finally, with buttons uncovered, Bulgarian papers substituted for Danish in my wallet, and my cap, complete with badge, set at what I hoped was a suitably rakish Slav angle, I stepped out onto an empty and deserted platform.

From my journey to the camp nine months earlier I remembered my way to the main station. Arrived there, I was faced by a fresh problem. There were two entrances, civilian and military. Which should I use, and ought I to buy my ticket before or after entering? Eventually I decided to try the military way in, but was stopped at the barrier and asked for my papers and ticket. I played dumb—in the American sense—and merely handed in my letter of introduction, saying *"Nicht Deutsch."* The guard read it through, nodding his head and saying, *"Ja"* to himself. Finally, he decided that "benevolent assistance" was indicated, and a minion was sent to help me. This worthy escorted me along to the book-

The "Bulgarian" Naval Officer

ing office, bought me a third-class ticket to Lübeck, found out the time and platform of departure of my train, and finally took me to the waiting room and ordered me a beer!

I was so bewildered by these developments that it took me some time to calm down. I could not but be most encouraged. Evidently my papers were going to see me through most difficulties, while my uniform appeared to be causing no comment. As a final test, I went up to a German sailor at the next table and asked him for the loan of a knife. He handed it to me without a word, and, German fashion, I brought a loaf of bread out of my case and cut off a large hunk.

Escaping is rather like that embarrassing social situation when you meet someone who evidently knows you well but whom you cannot place. Luckily, having a shocking memory for names and faces, I have had plenty of practice at pretending to know and then asking innocent leading questions, such as "How long would it be since we last met?" until I get a clue. Traveling through an enemy country—and I had never been to Germany before—is like this on a vast scale. Without ever appearing ignorant, I had to learn the currency, what was and what wasn't rationed, whether one tipped the waiter, and lots of other points. Having so far paid for everything with a ten-mark note, I took my change along to the "Gentlemen's" to see what the various coins were. Here another question arose. Should I put a penny in the slot or give it to the attendant? Eventually I did the latter, and spent the next half hour learning which coin was which.

I caught the 4:17 train to Hamburg and arrived there without incident just after 6 P.M. Again ignorance led me into trouble. As one of the great junctions of the country and the main artery across the Elbe, Hamburg Station had some very sharp-eyed police about. It would have been possible for me to go from the Bremen to the Lübeck platform without going through a barrier at all, but not knowing the station layout, I left the platform at the wrong end and had to pass through three control points. One of these was a wicked place—a constriction in a passage, painted white and lighted by arc-lights, in which stood three Gestapo officials scrutinizing everyone who passed. I felt a lot better when I was through; for the fact that I was not stopped meant that I must have fitted in pretty well with my surroundings.

The waiting room was packed, chiefly with soldiers on leave. I really felt quite sorry hanging my dear old naval cap up beside the Nazi ones with their high, stiff brims. It was like leaving a friend alone among thieves.

One could at that time still get a coupon-free dish in all German restaurants at lunch- and dinnertime. This dish, called the "*Stamm*," was usually only a bowl of vegetable soup, but for a few days I thought it should be sufficient to keep my stomach full.

Sitting at the next table to me as I ate was a young soldier with an Afrika Korps flash on his shoulder. I suspect that he had seen a Royal Navy uniform before, for he kept on looking at me very strangely. I returned his gaze, and he evidently lacked the courage of his convictions, for he never came up to me.

When I left to catch my 8 P.M. train for Lübeck, I was stopped at the barrier and asked for my papers. The man just looked at my identity card, said "*'s gut*," and let me go on. It struck me as rather amusing that he should accept without question a document in Bulgarian lettering. Only the serial number and the photograph were intelligible to a Western European, and the latter bore very little resemblance to me.

In the compartment of the Lübeck train, which was without light, a soldier and a civilian sat discussing the bombing. I was surprised at the open way they spoke, with a uniformed stranger in their midst, and soon after we pulled out of Hamburg they asked for my views of the situation. I explained that as a Bulgarian only recently arrived in the country, I hardly felt entitled to an opinion, and then took the opportunity to ask where there was a good place in Lübeck to sleep; for I was due to arrive just before midnight and did not fancy spending the night in the open.

They explained with emphasis that it was not safe to spend the night in any large German town in case of air raids. Was I due to go on any farther? Yes, I intended going to Stettin the following day. Without giving me a chance to explain that I had business in Lübeck first, the civilian said that he, too, was going to Stettin, and that he would show me a very nice station waiting room where he himself intended spending the night. Further, at the next stop, he would see the guard and buy me a supplementary ticket. Feeling it better to let sleeping dogs lie than to embark on long and tedious explanations, I agreed to this.

We duly passed Lübeck, and an hour later arrived at Bad Kleinen, the junction stop for Wismar. Here my friend bade me get out and led me to what was a reasonably comfortable waiting room, full of sleeping travelers. We found a vacant bench and sat down, but for me it was not to sleep. It had been an extraordinary day. Fourteen hours previously I had been in the camp; now I was the best of two hundred miles away and on a coast full of promise. If I played my cards properly, I should be home in a few weeks! . . . or possibly even days. . . .

At about 6 A.M. the next day, I caught a train on to Stettin. It was fearfully crowded and ran very late. My compartment was full of soldiers of the young Nazi breed—swaggering and making far too much noise. At 9 A.M. there was a long halt just outside a place called Pasewalk. The carriage was getting stifling, but I looked at my watch with a certain sly satisfaction. Any minute now Tubby would be walking complacently to *Appell* (roll call) and the *Feldwebel* would go up and salute smartly and say: "One man missing.". . .

It was after 1 P.M. when we finally reached Stettin and I was beginning to feel very hungry, but with only three hours of daylight left there was no time to waste, so I set off in search of ships. Stettin must be by far the ugliest of all the Baltic ports but it was exciting to be there, and for a seaman it was enough just to be beside a river again, with tugs and ferryboats bustling about. Moreover, I was convinced that at any moment I was going to find a Swedish ship that would take me to freedom.

A couple of hours' walking speedily changed this view. I could find no free harbor, as I had supposed, and what ships I could see were German and in inaccessible positions. Actually I know now that my search was incomplete. To find the docks in a large town without the aid of some map or plan is no easy task. I naturally searched the main riverbanks from the west (or railway station) side; I did not know that had I crossed the main bridge I should have found extensive free quays two miles to the eastward, connecting with the main river farther downstream.

As it grew dusk, therefore, my spirits fell, and I became convinced that Stettin was no use. David Jolly—the only man I knew who had been there before—had drawn blank and so had I. The one redeeming feature was that I had walked around the harbor for five hours without anyone commenting on my uniform. I became yet more confident in the disguise, even though I despaired of finding a ship.

To cheer myself up, I went on a combined *Stamm*-and-pub crawl. At each of six waterfront pubs I had a bowl of soup and one or two half-liters of beer, at the same time keeping my ears open for any sound of Scandinavian being spoken.

A strange thing about some of these cafés was the little placard hung up in the bar saying, "*Wir grüssen hier mit Heil Hitler.*" Fancy an English pub having to display a notice saying, "The motto of this house is God save the King!" In any case I took the hint and thoroughly enjoyed clicking my heels and saying, "*Heil Hitler*" with arm raised in every establishment I entered. By the time I reached the station, I was taking a much brighter view of life, and even thought, as I had ample funds, of taking a train to Switzerland for a spot of skiing.

Finally, I resolved to try one more Baltic port, and took a second-class ticket to Lübeck. As the scheme of sleeping in a midway waiting room had worked so well the previous night, I decided to try it again, and chose a place called Neu-Brandenburg, well known as a prison camp in the war of 1914–18. On alighting, I mingled with a crowd of naval enlisted men and made for the waiting room. We were just trying to open the door when an

The "Bulgarian" Naval Officer

RTO came up and told us that there was better accommodation for servicemen in the *Wehrmachtsunterkunft* (a German armed forces canteen), and ushered us firmly along there.

The place was certainly pleasant enough. A buxom Red Cross nurse gave us soup and coffee free; we found a fire and a number of comfortable chairs in which to sleep. But it was no place for a British naval officer. There was a German naval officer sitting at the next table, and with him were about a dozen sailors. It was all very well to get away with it in the street, but sitting opposite them all night was a very different matter. Still, I could not very well leave, so I had perforce to continue playing my part. As soon as one of them started to doze off, I began to nod. Of course, any idea of sleep was out of the question, but it was the most convincing part to play. . . . Crash! . . . What was that? . . . I looked at my watch. It was six o'clock and the last sailor was going through the door. What extraordinary things occur! Entirely against my wishes I had spent a night in full uniform alongside an officer of the *Kriegsmarine* (the German Navy), and in official military accommodation too, and nobody had recognized me!

A few minutes later I was in the train rattling on toward Lübeck. By this time I was beginning to take rail travel for granted, but this was the one journey that caused me some embarrassment. A garrulous old man was sitting opposite, and he kept on quoting what sounded like proverbs or clichés at me in Low German. I could not understand a word he said, so smiled merrily and answered *"Ja"* or *"Nein,"* as seemed best. Then I got up and gave my seat to an old lady. No sooner had I done so than I realized that it was not "the thing to do." People looked at me as though I were some creature from a strange world observing different customs. To make matters worse, I was jammed up against some little Hitler Youths. I was always terrified of children. They are so quick-witted and observant. The ordinary man is not usually "up" in types of aircraft, enemy uniforms, and the like, but it is just the sort of information on which little boys thrive. These lads only came up to my chest; I was frightened lest they should see the London stamp on the inner side of my service buttons.

But the time passed, and shortly after 11 A.M. we arrived at Lübeck. My first need was for a shave, so by way of an experiment I went into a barber's shop and asked for one. It was an almost fatal blunder; for, as far as I could understand him, the man told me that, with soap rationing, there had been no shaves for about two years, and who was I to know so little about things anyway. Muttering *"Ach so,"* I left hurriedly, followed by many a curious glance.

It is a strange fact that although all my time at large in Germany was during good weather, in retrospect it seems as though the sun never shone. Everything there was so dull and cheerless, I can only visualize it beneath skies of gray. Other escapers have returned with exactly the same impression.

Lübeck was the only exception. A charming little town, it seemed a sort of backwater from the mainstream of war—there was more in the shops, the people seemed better dressed and more cheerful, and—yes, the sun shone. Just over the bridge was a comfortable hotel, and to this I went for my shave. The porter's desk was empty, so I locked myself in a bathroom, had a good wash, and put on a clean shirt and collar. I felt much better after that, and went down to the restaurant for lunch.

This meal was notable for the well-dressed people there—one couple in particular could have been transported straight to the Berkeley—and also for a two-course *Stamm,* the only one I have ever heard of—a bowl of consommé, followed by a dry vegetable hash. This was the one trace of civilization I saw in the whole of Germany, and it made me long all the more for home.

Leaving my suitcase at the hotel, I started off on a reconnaissance in high hopes. If the geography of Stettin was hard, that of Lübeck was very easy, for here the river was flanked on either side by quays and warehouses, and these were the docks. Rather than walk down the verge between the warehouses and

The "Bulgarian" Naval Officer

the ships, where I might conceivably have got picked up for taking too great an interest in the goings-on, I decided to use the road outside, which was full of trucks, dockers, horses, and carts, and cover the opposite bank by peering through the occasional gaps between the warehouses. Taking the east bank first, I walked about two miles and, to my great excitement, saw two Swedish ships. That meant that they were still trading to Germany and were not shut in by Baltic ice, as I was beginning to fear. On the other hand, they were not of much use to me, since they were both auxiliary schooners, with decks piled high with lumber, so that, quite apart from the lack of good hiding room there is in a sailing ship, they might be several days yet in discharging their cargoes.

Retracing my steps, therefore, to the main bridge over the river, I started to walk down the west bank, looking east.

Almost at once I saw just what I was after—two coasters lying alongside, bow to stern, with Swedish flags painted on their topsides. For the first quarter mile below the bridge the river was divided into two by a long, narrow spit or peninsula, called the *Halbinsel.* and it was alongside this that they lay.

Without further ado, I turned for the hotel to get my bag. Since it was thirty-one hours since I had last been challenged, and as a bold and forward policy had always worked hitherto, I resolved to try to walk aboard in broad daylight, trusting that an authoritative bearing and decisive manner would prevent anyone from asking me my business.

It was after three o'clock when I left the hotel, and I was glad that things were going to be put to the test. I was beginning to feel the lack of food and sleep; also, one operates the whole time under certain nervous tension, and I wanted to get the matter settled one way or the other.

As I approached the *Halbinsel,* I found that it was wired off with a gate and a sentry. This latter, however had a beat nearly thirty yards long; for a road and a double railway track ran onto the peninsula through the gap he was guarding in the wire. Better still, there were some goods vans on one of the tracks, jutting out just beyond the line of his beat.

My line of approach lay along the main road and bridge, cutting across the *Halbinsel*, with the wire on my right hand. I adjusted my pace so that the sentry would have his back to me—that is, be walking in the same direction as I—by the time I reached the goods wagons. When he turned at the near end of his beat, I was just walking down the road, apparently interested in a girl on the pavement opposite; twelve paces later I had dodged down the track behind the goods vans.

I came onto the jetty, and there, ahead of me, lay the two Swedish ships. There were no sentries on the gangway, but I could not afford to hesitate. A quick glance—they both looked exactly the same—and I made for the nearer, which was loading coal. In a fever of excitement that can well be imagined, I walked straight up the gangplank. In front of me lay a companionway, so I went down it. Below, I found myself in an alleyway with doors on either side. I saw one marked "Steward," knocked and went straight in.

A pleasant, sandy-haired individual looked up as I entered. "Excuse me, I'm an escaped British officer and I'm in need of help. . . ." A pause. . . . He got up, went over and locked the door.

So far so good. I began to have dreams of home by Christmas. He produced a cigar and a drink and asked me how I had got there. I gave him the outline of my story, and asked in return why he had demanded no proof of my identity.

"Oh, I recognized your uniform. I spent the first two years of the war trading on the English coast."

After three days of furtive wandering, with nobody to talk to, it was a relief to be able to gossip quite freely with this man! The precious minutes began to slip by. . . .

"And now to business, Steward. I want to get to Sweden. Can you hide me away anywhere?"

"Sure. Just you wait here and I'll go and arrange it with the

Chief Engineer." A few minutes later he came back with a long face. "It's no good. The Chief says that she is low on coal and due to bunker tomorrow. That means there will be stevedores crawling about the ship everywhere. Your best plan is to go to the ship astern. She's a motorship belonging to the same company, and she's due to sail today some time. Her steward is a good fellow—took some Russians to Gothenburg last trip. Offer to make it worth his while and he'll certainly hide you away."

I argued the point. I felt so secure aboard this ship that I was loath to leave her, even for a fifty-yard walk down the jetty, but at length the steward persuaded me it was the best thing to do.

I had to wait a minute at the bottom of the companionway while a bulky individual, evidently the skipper, came below. When I reached the deck they were casting off ropes on the jetty. As I watched, the gap between the other ship and the wall slowly grew. Was it worth making a dash for it? Obviously not. A pier-head jump would cause far too much attention. Even if there was no police or a pilot aboard, some bystander would certainly report the occurrence and she would be stopped farther down the ten-mile river. No, I had missed her, and that by seconds.

I returned to my steward friend, who went on deck to see for himself. When he came back he had already made up his mind. "It is no use your staying here," he said. "You will be in greater danger than if you are ashore. Have you money?"

"Yes."

"Well, stay away till Monday. If you come back, I'll take you to Gothenburg. Till then, the best of luck to you."

A moment's thought. There was obviously some force to his arguments, and anyway I could not well run him into trouble. It had been quite easy getting into the dockyard area; it should be no harder to get out. Yes, I had better go. My hopes were still high as I left the ship. I had got my passage arranged. I could spend Sunday taking a trip up to Rostock for a look around in case there was anything better.

My return route was at right angles to the sentry's beat. I

tried to time it to pass the danger zone when his back was turned but I was just too late. As I walked away down the road, a voice shouted after me, "*Halt!*" I turned, trying to look as innocent and indignant as I could.

"What were you doing in the dockyard?"

"Seeing off a friend; the mate of that ship that has just left."

"Where are your papers and dockyard pass? What, you have no pass? Then you must come with me to the guardhouse."

I was taken there, and an escort was provided to take me to Battalion Headquarters. The Duty Officer was impressed with my papers and with my protests at the indignity of arresting a distinguished allied officer. He explained to me that it was his duty to check up on me since I had no pass. Could he look in my case?

As there was nothing incriminating in it, I showed it to him readily enough. He went out for a few minutes and held a conversation next door. When he returned, it was to say that the *Kommandant* thought it would be best for me to go to the police station: "Just to get everything regulated." It was a suggestion admitting of no refusal, and as my only possible line I agreed with outward enthusiasm, but with a sinking feeling within. My chances of fooling the professional police were slim —and the stories one heard of the German police were not encouraging. . . .

We arrived at a building on the waterfront marked "*Wasserschutzpolizei*." They were, I suppose, the German equivalent of a river police force. Thank God it was not the Gestapo, anyway!

A fat, red-faced man listened while my escort told his tale; then, turning to me, he asked for my identity card. I gave it to him, and made a vigorous protest against being arrested. Paying no attention, he went over to a cupboard and took out a magnifying glass. After scrutinizing the card for a minute, he looked up and said, "Where did you escape from?" The game was obviously up, but I said stiffly, "I am afraid I don't know what you mean." He replied, "Yes, you know perfectly well."

The "Bulgarian" Naval Officer

I gave him my full name, rank and camp, and produced my identity disk in support. His first action was to call in a junior, and together they congratulated the man who had arrested me. He was naturally delighted, and stood looking on with a grin from ear to ear. He, too, probably had visions of being home for Christmas.

The red-faced man showed the other my pass, and then, turning to me, said scornfully: "How did you expect to leave Germany on a rotten pass like that?"

Before I could reply, the other cut in and said, "Not at all. When you think of what few facilities they possess in those camps, it's a very fine bit of work." Turning to me, he pointed at the stamp of the Chief of Police, Cologne, and said, "Look, that is your one bad mistake. You've put 'Polizei Kommissar.' It should be 'Polizei Präsident.'"

I was searched for weapons and asked to make a statement. I had no intention of playing around with the German police, so I made one, substantially true, but lying on all key points. They cannot have known anything about camp life, for they wrote down quite happily that I had walked out of the main gate at dusk when the sentry was not looking!

I had a strong desire—presumably a sort of defense mechanism —to boast of my time at large, and I derived the greatest pleasure from telling them of my night in the *Wehrmachtsunterkunft* at Neu-Brandenburg. The man with the red face grew yet redder, and there were broad grins on the faces of the rest. The news of my capture seemed to have spread, for quite a number of others had come in to see the specimen. Baiting Red-Face in front of such an appreciative audience was great fun. . . .

I was asked how I had got into the prohibited zone. Not without a certain feeling of satisfaction, I turned and pointed at my captor. "Past him, when his back was turned." Broad grin quickly vanished.

"At what time?"

"About three ten."

To the sentry: "Were you on duty then?"

Sentry: "Yes."

One of the police went over to the telephone and rang up the commanding officer. I would not be the only man in jail over Christmas!

The questions being finished, the nasty one left the room. The younger man immediately offered me a cigarette, and I in return shared the rest of my chocolate with him.

A few minutes later he was detailed off to escort me to the local military jail. On the way there he informed me that the camp had been told of my recapture and would fetch me in a couple of days. He added as a rider to this that he was sorry, personally, that I had had such bad luck.

Taking advantage of his friendliness, I said, "I suppose, of course, that you knew I was at large?"

"Naturally," he said. "We had a full description of you in the office yesterday."

It was a lie. Why, I had to write my name out for them and spell the address of the camp. It would be useful for future reference to know that the Baltic ports were not informed when we were at large. I'd have to try that route again sometime.

It was dark when we arrived at the military jail. Again I was searched, and my name and rank were put in a large register, but I was allowed to keep my small case and all my gear. A jailer led me along a dark passage till we came to a massive door. It was opened for me, and I entered a small cell. Behind me the door clanged, and, worn out, I fell onto the hard bed and went to sleep. . . .

. . . David James was unlucky that time, but he was not the man to give up. He took his punishment for attempting to escape and within a couple of months he was out again—by exactly the same method. This time he traveled as a merchant seaman and succeeded in stowing away on a ship bound for Sweden.

5.

Crossing the Border

George Millar is the author of two exciting books about life among French Resistance workers in the last war. He was captured by the Germans in the Western Desert in 1942 and handed over to the Italians, who took him to a prison camp in Italy. Later he was transferred to a monastery camp at Padula from which he made several attempts to escape. As a punishment he was sent to a "naughty boys' camp"—Campo V at Gavi, which was an ancient fortress.

George Millar had not long been in Campo V when Italy capitulated and the Germans took over the Allied prisoners. With the new guards, who did not know the fort, escape attempts were redoubled, and when the Germans gave the order to leave for Germany in half an hour, Millar hid, in the hope of being left behind. But the Germans were very thorough in their search, and he was discovered and sent to Germany with the others.

On the journey to a permanent camp in Germany, George Millar and another prisoner, Wally Binns, jumped from the train and made contact with a party of French prisoners from a work-

ing camp. These Frenchmen, who were employed on the railway in Munich, fed and clothed the two escapers and stowed them away in a train destined for Strasbourg on the French border. In Strasbourg Binns became separated from Millar, who was befriended by a group of anti-German Italians. They fitted him out with clothes and false papers and passed him on to Paris.

After more adventures and many narrow escapes, George Millar made contact with a British agent working with the Resistance and was passed along an escape line to Perpignan on the Spanish border. He made two false starts (one with a guide named Pedro, who was later killed) before setting out with a band of American evaders to cross the Pyrenees into Spain. It was January, the worst time for such a mountain crossing, and the American airmen were out of training through lying hidden for so long. . . .

. . . Eight o'clock the following night found us once more at the corner of the plowed field outside Perpignan where we had met Pedro.

The guide this time was a small, wizened man with a very high voice that had a hollow, conchlike tone. He spoke only the Catalan tongue, with a sprinkling of French, but thanks to my sketchy knowledge of Italian, I clearly understood him. There was another man with him, a tall, husky fellow who smelled strongly of wine. This man carried an enormous knapsack, which clinked when he covered rough ground, and which probably contained contraband in the shape of bottles of alcohol or perfume.

Our little guide gave no melodramatic instructions with regard to dogs. He only asked me to advise the Americans to relax as much as possible while they walked and to forget that they were covering the ground, because from then until dawn they would be walking all the time.

"How can we forget?—Ask him that," said Charlie.

"Think of God, or a woman," replied the old man.

"Ask him how we cross the River Tech."

"We will cross nearer the sea than you did on your attempt

with the ill-fated Pedro, and you will see that it is not difficult. Only, I shall demand absolute silence, especially on the far bank, which is apt to be closely guarded."

He set off, padding smoothly in *espadrilles* down paths that we had followed with Pedro. If anything, this man was more cautious than Pedro, and we reached the first river in good time without causing a dog to bark. The Americans were thoroughly broken in by this time, and they were walking well, although I knew that their feet must hurt. Mine did.

The guide took off his shoes at the river, and waded in barefoot. I was glad, because I had earlier decided to do that in order to preserve my boots and make the walking more comfortable between streams. Also, the level of this stream was much lower than it had been when we were with Pedro.

He would not let us sit down for more than two or three minutes at a time.

"When you rest too much, your legs get stiff. Just sit long enough to relax all the muscles. Then walk on. That is the way."

He himself seemed to flow across the ground with tiny, smooth steps. Like Pedro, he carried a long stick. He said that he was fifty-five, but the assistant whispered, "The old one is vain, very vain, and likes to think that he is still young. He is sixty-five."

This time we reached the north bank of the Tech before midnight. The river looked wider and shallower at this point. The guide asked us to follow him at thirty-yard intervals in case the enemy saw us and began shooting. The water was terribly cold and the stones cut our feet. I counted 290 steps on the way across.

We sat down in dense undergrowth on the south bank and were drying ourselves and putting on trousers and boots and socks when a terrible shouting broke out. After a moment we realized what had happened. The old man had crossed first and had arrived farther downstream. His assistant had followed him, and all of us had followed the assistant. Now the old man (who had demanded absolute silence) could not find us, and was screaming insults at the assistant, who answered in kind.

When we linked up with him ten minutes later, three of the Americans had got lost. There was more shouting until they arrived.

We walked on into the forbidden zone. We had not gone far when the old guide stopped so suddenly that we all cannoned into him. Three figures were crossing a field toward us. In a flurry the guide turned, barged his way through the Americans, and dashed back along the path we had been following. We all followed him in a mad rush for some three hundred yards, when he cut off to the left down another track. He made a big circle, and soon we were on our original path.

By this time the Pyrenees were coming closer. But the closeness was deceptive. To get to the mountains, it was necessary for us to act as counters in some diabolical game of "Snakes and Ladders." The rungs in our ladder were rivers that had to be waded or roads that had to be stalked and then crawled across. The guide was most careful with the roads. At one of them he turned to me and whispered, "I once lost a bottle of Napoleon brandy here. A German bicycle patrol came around that corner just as I was crossing. I ran so fast that I left the bottle behind."

"Was it real Napoleon brandy?"

"Of course not. It never is. But it was marked clearly on the bottle, and it would have fetched a Napoleon price in Spain. I won it at bowling: the bottle, I mean. The brandy I had put in from something a little newer and more shapely in the way of bottles."

We began climbing when we came to the olive groves. It was hard work on the terraced ground. Then we left the olives and climbed up woodland paths. At one of our short halts I took off Pedro's oiled silk coat, which I had carried in a roll over one shoulder. I took it off to make a seat on the damp ground. And when we went on, I forget it. That forgetfulness might have cost me my life.

At 5 A.M. we cleared the woods, and the bare mountains were above us. The guide told us to sleep in some bushes while he and his assistant went to a cottage farther up the hill. We had been walking for nine hours. All of us went to sleep among the sparse bushes and were awakened by strange noises like the barking of a small lapdog. They were made by the guide.

"More climbing now," he said. "Fill your water bottles passing the cottage. I apologize for leaving you outside. But there are often German patrols here. If they found us, they would take us for visiting shepherds. If they found you, they would kill everybody, burn the cottage, torture my friend's wife, and eat his sheep."

At the back door of the cottage a thin woman, wearing a jacket of sheepskin and trousers of some soft leather, filled our bottles with earthy-tasting water. Then we went on climbing up a narrow path over and through big rocks. Often tough thornbushes closed behind the man in front, lashing those who followed with tearing branches. It was bitterly cold, although we could see a strong-looking sun beginning to rise over the sea horizon. We were tired, but would have liked to go on climbing to keep warm. At eight o'clock, however, the guide said that it was getting dangerously light.

He shepherded us into the thorn-scrub below the mountain path.

"You will enjoy several hours of sunshine here today," he said. "Tell your friends that if they get a good sleep and eat solidly in the evening, they should be in Spain tomorrow morning. Warn them not to drink too much water, because that is bad for crossing the mountains, and this crossing is never easy in winter. My friend and I are going back to sleep the day away in the cottage below. *Au revoir*, and don't move about. That big house down there is the headquarters of the German frontier guards. They occasionally send patrols over the hills during the daytime, and some of them have dogs."

I faithfully transmitted his instructions to the Americans. They had borne up bravely all through the night. Now they seemed to have an enormous thirst. Before the end of the morning, all our water had been drunk. I attributed their thirst to their unfit condition. The one we had called Clark Gable looked quite ill. He lay near me, heavily asleep, his face a greenish gray against his mossy pillow.

The air at that height was cold and crisp, even when the sun was on our hill face. A heavy coastal battery of German guns had firing practice during the afternoon. The shells fell a long way out to sea. The guns themselves were sited nearly a mile inland.

From our high resting place we could see all our little milestones of the past three weeks stretched out below us in a huge relief map. We could see Perpignan, the first river, the Tech, and the subsequent rivers. There were the two roads making a wishbone forking toward us from Perpignan. And down below us, where the hills ran into the sea, lay Port Vendres, such a dramatic little port in the Spanish Civil War. Pale wisps of wood smoke rose from its distant chimneys against the pale winter blue of the Mediterranean.

Although I could not sleep, I ate all that I carried and lay as relaxed as possible on the slope. At the beginning of this attempt I had not had enough money to buy provisions. I had left Perpignan with two tins of French Army meat, two small loaves, and one of the cakes that Serge and I had bought for the second attempt. The Americans wondered to see me finish my provisions, but I told them that it was better to have a full stomach before we set off on the worst part of the journey than to save up for a meal when we were across.

Within myself I felt an immense exultation, for I was convinced that in twenty-four hours I should be safe from the Germans.

The guides arrived promptly at five, but we had to wait until six before the old man considered it dark enough for us to begin climbing. The early going was good on a bare, rocky path.

We stopped at a spring to fill all our water bottles. While we were there, three of the Americans got down on their knees and

Crossing the Border

lapped at the water like dogs. When he saw this, the guide stood on a rock above them and jabbered at them in his high voice.

"Bad, bad, bad. Water is bad on the hills. Much better drink wine." He offered his wineskin, but nobody felt like drinking wine.

The guide now wore a kind of fluffy woolen helmet, which covered all but his sharp nose and his restless eyes. He led us up small paths made perhaps by goats, perhaps by men. Sometimes he left the paths to slither across steep hill faces. He explained that he did this to avoid German posts, which were often placed on the high ground.

A bitter north wind cut into our backs. I deeply regretted the loss of Pedro's coat, for even with the climbing I could not keep warm.

"This wind is the tramontane," said the guide. "It will get much worse and it will bring snow."

"Tonight?"

"When else?"

We had been walking and climbing for two hours and a half when we stopped to rest in a small dark pinewood. All of the Americans were extremely tired and had sore feet.

"Of what do they speak?" asked the guide.

"They speak of the possibilities of victory next year," I lied.

"I know that they are talking about their tired limbs. That is because they have drunk too much water. Tell them they drink no more water. Let them ask for wine. Eh, *amigo*, pass your skin."

His companion passed the wine with some grumbling, and this time we all drank, including the guide himself.

"Tell your comrades to have courage, for with courage man conquers all," he continued with a chuckle. "Tell them I lost my brother here one year ago."

My translation of his morbid injunction was met by hollow groans from the Americans, for their extreme fatigue could not yet prevent them from laughing at everything, including themselves.

After this rest we slithered down a hill so steep that it just failed to be a precipice. At the bottom was a raging torrent, which had to be crossed by leaping from boulder to boulder. Two of the Americans, Gable, and one nicknamed Chauve-Souris (Bat), fell heavily but followed on. The Chauve-Souris had been lagging for some time.

We had not, it appeared, traversed the main block of the mountains, and we turned west, paralleling what the guide said was the last ridge before the Spanish frontier. This paralleling was the most arduous work of all, for there were continual high ridges running across our path, so that we were like some infinitely small animals climbing in and out of the squares of a giant honeycomb. Now, too, we were walking in snow, although it was not deep enough to present much of a handicap.

I explained to the Americans that we were working along the high ridge on our left, keeping well below the summit because there were German frontier posts and patrols there, and that the guide would turn up it at a place where he knew it would be safe to cross. But an exhausted man finds it difficult to reason and easy to complain. Our line grew more and more strung out. The guide frequently had to halt to allow the Chauve-Souris, Charlie, and Gable to catch up. I would have liked to push on much faster, for it was the cold, not fatigue, that worried me. My back was freezing in the tramontane.

Charlie told me at one point that he had seen cows and I thought he must be going mad.

"Can't you tell a cow from a goat?"

But a little later I saw them myself, a large, half-wild herd of small cows. And I suddenly remembered an Alpine climber talking with scorn of the Pyrenees as *"montagnes des vaches."*

The blizzard became so bad and so heavy with wet snow that the guide led us into a small cave in the hillside. Here there was just room for all of us to rest, squeezed together and dripping water from our soaking clothes. The others smoked. Some shepherd had left a crude oil lamp there. The guide lit it and I was able to look at my companions.

My heart would have bled for them had I been less intent on surmounting this final obstacle. Except for Fritz, who seemed to thrive on the work, they were plainly in the last stages of exhaustion.

Gable, the biggest and toughest-looking of us all, told me that he could not go much farther.

"Why not?"

"My legs are passing out on me."

The Chauve-Souris and Charlie seemed to be equally miserable. The Trapper was little better, although he complained less since he came from tougher, less citified, stock.

They begged me to ask the guide if we could either stop there for the night or if he could take us by a quick, direct route to the frontier.

"If we wait here, we shall die from the cold," he answered. "I must take you by the proper route. Tell them it is only one hour from here to the frontier if this blizzard dies down, as I think it will very soon."

The going was more difficult when we started out again, and the Americans, excepting Fritz, were slower than ever. At one short halt, when the guide left us for a moment to look at the crest of the ridge, Gable lay down on a patch of snow and shouted, "I can't go on, I can't go on."

Fritz and I went back to him.

"My legs have given out," he said. "Ask the old man if he can give us five minutes' rest."

"Certainly not," said the guide indignantly. "Tell him to be a man."

He now noticed that some of them were stuffing lumps of snow into their mouths. For although it was deathly cold and eerie and wet on the mountaintop, we were parched with thirst. "If you drink like that you will die," shrieked the guide.

So we moved on slowly to what he said was the last slope. It was very steep, and the snow was deeper and softer. The four weak Americans were in grave difficulties. Fritz and I had to divide all that they carried between us. They struggled bravely at the slope. But there were times when they all lay down in the bitter cold, and we despaired of ever getting them over.

The guide and his assistant did nothing to help. They only got angry, screaming at us and jabbering in fast, incomprehensible Catalan. I have never given so many encouraging discourses in such a short time. They sounded false to me, up there in the whistling wind, and they had little effect on Gable, who, poor soul, was now almost unconscious with pain from his failing legs. The others somehow, little by little, managed to drag themselves up. The Trapper and Charlie hung together and kept going inch by inch with a rest every few yards. The Chauve-Souris, brave spirit, negotiated the whole slope on hands and knees. This left the two of us to deal with Gable.

At first he lay on the snow saying, "I can't, I tell you."

Fritz gave him a "You're doing fine, boy," piece of nonsense.

Gable responded by walking with our help for twenty yards, then he sank down again. While he lay there, Fritz talked to him and the Chauve-Souris passed us, crawling. I was reminded of the hare and the tortoise and burst out laughing. The old guide chose this moment to come back and scream that this was the most dangerous part of the whole trip.

"Kick him into activity. Does he want to kill us all?"

"Ask him to let me rest here for a half hour, just a half hour," moaned Gable, his voice trailing away slowly in a sleepy drawl.

"Rest?" yelled the guide (I had not dared to translate the 'half-hour' request). "Rest? I'll give him rest, the pig."

He danced down the slope and slapped Gable sharply several times on the face. This roused the poor man, and, supported by Fritz and me, he did another fifty yards.

Then he collapsed finally. Fritz and I tried everything we could think of—praise, vilification, encouragement, massage, wine from the Spaniard's skin, alcohol from Fritz's little bottle. The big man would not move. Tears oozed from his eyes.

"Leave me here to die, you fellows. I can't go on."

The Chauve-Souris passed us again, going bravely on hands and knees. I pointed him out to Gable.

The only comment this drew was, "Just give me a half-hour and I think I'll be okay."

Charlie and the Trapper were nearly over the ridge. The guide and his assistant were ahead of them. The Chauve-Souris was nearing the top.

Fritz and I managed to raise big Gable. He sagged. We each got a shoulder under him, twining his heavy thick arms like dead pythons round our straining necks. We gathered ourselves together and managed to stagger up to the top and over the ridge. He kept saying maddening things like, "Let me be, fellows. Just let me rest."

The summit of the ridge was narrow and smooth; below it lay a few yards of scrub, then stunted pine trees. The three of us fell in a heap. I lay there with the blood pounding in my ears.

When I picked myself up, Gable again was asking for "a half-hour rest."

Fritz and I worked on him. We ran the full gamut at first aid, we talked to him lovingly, angrily. Nothing happened. The other three lay around us in the scrub, offering advice. The two Spaniards stood sourly under a tree, watching us. Occasionally, the guide hurled piping invective at us. At last he came over to look at the prostrate giant.

"The Spanish frontier is thirty minutes' easy walking from here," he said. "We go down to the burn below us, over it, up on the other side, and then across the plateau. At the far edge of the plateau is the frontier, and you can see the lights of the Spanish town of Figueras from there."

"Why don't you leave me, then?" said Gable. "I'll make it when my legs get some strength back in them."

"We won't leave you. You must come with us now. It's too cold to lie here."

"I'll cover myself with leaves. See . . ." He began to scrabble leaves over his legs. "After an hour or two I'll go on down to Spain. Now I got to get some rest. . . ."

"Enough of this foolery," screamed the guide. "I have been taking men across all this winter and I never saw such women.

This is the worst part. Sooner or later, Germans will pass here. Are you all going to throw your chance away for one weakling?"

He suddenly darted on Gable.

"I will *make* you go on," he shouted. Before we could stop him, he seized two handfuls of Gable's black hair and began to bash his big head against a tree trunk. Gable only moaned gently.

"I don't care what you do to me. I can't go on."

When I had translated the guide's remarks about German patrols to him, he only replied, "What do I care about Germans? My legs hurt so badly. Please go on without me. I'll be okay. I see the way. You none of you'll make it if you take me along. It's the only hope, to leave me. When I've rested I'll go on down into Spain. . . ."

After all the ground that had been covered I could practically see the Spanish frontier. After the help of Wally Binns, the French prisoners, the Strasbourg café plotters, Ramón and Alban, Greta, Scherb, Dolores, Pascal, La Pepelte, Xavier, Elizabeth, Clément, Laurence, Serge, Estève, Cartelet—after all that, I was stuck here, almost within jumping distance of the frontier. Stuck, stuck, stuck! Because one American had been too lazy to do three deep knee bends each day that he was hidden up in Paris. Was my duty to this man, or to all that lay behind me and all that lay ahead?

I could not decide. I asked Fritz.

"I reckon we should leave him, as he asks. He may make it in the morning. If we stop here, it may mean all of us get lost."

I asked the Trapper, Charlie, and the Chauve-Souris. They were all of the same opinion as Fritz. By this time the guide, who did not understand what this talk was about, was screaming, "To perdition with you all, you bunch of women! I am going on. I will not throw myself away for you. . . ."

We covered Gable's body with leaves and left him what food and wine remained. We showed him the road to the frontier again.

The others moved off. He had relaxed, and looked much better now that he knew he was to be allowed to rest. When I was hurrying after the others, I bumped into a man in the darkness.

Crossing the Border

"Who is it?"

"It's me," said the Chauve-Souris. "Listen, Lieutenant. I was in the same house with him for six months in Paris. I'm going to stay with him. Furthermore, my legs are just about all in too, and I would be a drag on the rest of the party. I could never make the frontier tonight. We'll go on down together in the daylight. See you in Spain...."

"Keep each other awake," I told him. "It's too cold, dangerously cold, to go to sleep. If you go to sleep, you may never wake. Drink all the wine and eat the food. Rub each other's legs and get on down as soon as you feel you can move. I'm glad you're staying with him. It's a good thing to do. A decent thing . . ." But already we had separated in the wood, and I was running down toward the burn (brook), after the others.

The Trapper and Charlie were both in a bad way, and the effort of carrying Gable had taken a lot out of Fritz and me. We worked our way slowly up the wooded slope beyond the burn. There seemed to be a numbness in my legs. The guide was nervous and ill at ease. He repeatedly hissed at us to be silent or to hurry.

At last we came out on the plateau. It looked unnatural, like the face of the moon. The bitter wind swept across it, bludgeoning us forward, stabbing us forward. The guide nudged me and pointed to a kind of hillock at the far edge of the plateau.

"Keep that on your left hand," he said. "It marks the Spanish frontier. But you must make them run across here. We are in full view. It's not far. Look. Only three hundred meters."

He and the other Spaniard began to run away in front of us.

"Run," I shouted. "That's the frontier. Run. Run."

The Trapper and Fritz ran on. Charlie was too tired. He stumbled after them. A wild exaltation gripped me, filled me, maddened me.

"Just three hundred yards now, Charlie boy," I shouted at him. "Run with me."

"I can't."

"Run. Run. Run."

I took him by the hand and pulled him as you might an unwilling child. The pair of us broke into a shambling trot. I pulled and the wind pushed. Charlie responded nobly. Our speed increased. We crossed the plateau; and suddenly we were running away with ourselves as we dropped over the edge of the plateau—into Spain.

But were we in Spain?

It was true that far below us, beyond the slope of the hills, stretched a great plain with splashes of light on it from towns and villages, startling splashes to eyes accustomed to wartime darkness. Louis had warned me, however, that we could not be certain that we were in Spain until we had actually descended to the plain itself. He had also hinted that the Spanish frontier guards might hand over to the Germans anybody whom they captured actually on the frontier.

When we stopped at a spring to fill our water bottles, I realized for the first time that I had seriously twisted my left knee, possibly when we had fallen with Gable. It was difficult to stand up again.

The spring was high up in the hills. I had doubts about my ability to walk far.

"How far to the farm?" I asked.

"A good fifteen kilometers [nine miles]," replied the guide.

"Is it certain that we are in Spain?"

"Certain. This is your first trip. I have been crossing these mountains for twenty-six years. But we must walk on, and fast, because here in Spain I am in more danger than in France. And you are all in danger too, at any rate in danger of going to Miranda jail and having your heads shaved and catching a dose of the pox."

"I'd a hell of a lot rather catch that then keep on walking," said Charlie when I had translated. But they did keep on, he and the Trapper, although their feet were raw and they were nearly dropping. Crossing the frontier seemed to have given them a

Crossing the Border

second wind, whereas for me there was emptiness and pain. True, every fifty yards I told myself that I was FREE, but my whole body seemed to be sagging, and the pain in my knee made me gasp for rest. After a time the guide noticed how lame I was, and he bound the knee up tightly with a crepe bandage.

Descending the hills on a good, wide, stony track, the tramontane came whistling down into our backs again, cutting into my kidneys. Despite the labor of walking, I was desperately cold and shivery. I imagined that I was coming down with some illness. Through the short temper and unreasonableness of fatigue we became very angry with the guide and his companion.

At one point, just before leaving the hills for the plain, the two of them dumped us in a small wood and went off "to see if there were any of the *Guardia Civil* in the neighborhood." They came back when we had shivered for a miserable hour, and we were positive that although they said that they had found no sign of the *Guardia Civil*, they had certainly found some good fellowship and much liquor, for of the latter they both smelled strongly.

The provident Spaniards had refueled their large wineskins, and the farther we progressed, the better-tempered they became. They were generous with their skins and I drank freely of the wine, which had a tart, resinous tang that murdered thirst.

When we were on the plain, the little man drove straight on for a time and then turned east toward the sea. Usually we were on tracks or small roads, but he avoided villages, and there were more icy streams to ford. The walk seemed endless.

It was 5 A.M. when we arrived in a large village and the Spaniards pushed us into an old cow shed.

"Wait here, please," the guide said. "There is a sale of wine in this village, and I can assure you that it is a village famous for its wine."

"But you cannot ask us to wait here. The floor is one meter deep in dung."

"Dung does not bite. And we go to buy wine not only for ourselves but also for you."

"Let us accompany you."

"My friend, you would have me hanged. But listen. Here I will meet my son, who will take the message to have you met by your friends from the British Consulate in Barcelona."

To pass the two hours that we waited in the dung, we ate a tin of sardines that Charlie carried in his pocket, and the remnants of the bread the three of them had brought from Perpignan. The Americans were all three in good spirits, though we speculated grimly on the fate of Gable and the Chauve-Souris, still up there in the cold wind.

Our Spaniards arrived, singing, and arm in arm. The guide began by hanging a large, full wineskin around my neck.

"This is my son," he said, presenting a dark young man in white shoes. "He has been in touch with your people, and tonight you will meet at ten o'clock a representative of the British Consulate. He has also arranged for you to have a splendid dinner today. Now we will continue our promenade, but ask your friends to be quiet, for there is much police vigilance about here."

We walked southeast for another two hours, and day was breaking when the guide stopped in a lane, pointed to a thicket of bushes and young trees on the left, and said, "You will be very comfortable in there."

"For how long?"

"Only a short while. Do not fret now."

Obediently we climbed through a fence and disposed ourselves about the thicket. The three Americans lay down to sleep. But my leg hurt me too much and the cold had bitten too deeply into the small of my back. I stamped to and fro in the thicket, working myself into a really bad temper. The guide's companion had remained in the lane, as though he were keeping guard on us. My movements evidently worried him.

"For the love of God, keep still," he hissed into the bushes.

"I refuse to keep still. I am too cold. How long are we to remain here?"

"All day."

"All day! I refuse to remain here all day. Are we not going to a farmhouse?"

Crossing the Border

"Yes, tonight. What is the matter?"

"I am freezing, and I think I am sick. If we must remain here, I will light a fire."

The Spaniard stood up and peered in at me. Finally he shrugged his shoulders.

"It is your own suggestion, so why not? And I will gladly help you," he said.

Fritz and I built shelter walls by hammering in long uprights and weaving brushwood, while the other three gathered wood. In this way we soon had a small enclosure, well sheltered from the piercing wind, and with an enormous fire in the middle.

I lay beside the fire and let the blessed heat soak into my back and my knee. All that remained in the way of food was French tinned meat, *singe*. We divided this into four portions, toasted it on long sticks, and ate it without bread. Then, having banked our fire, all four of us went to sleep. That was a lifesaving fire.

Soon after 4 P.M., I awoke. The others were sitting up, complaining of hunger. My leg was very stiff. Otherwise I was stronger. We recalled the guide's promise to give us a fine meal that day. We laughed at his promise.

But at 4:30 he arrived with two more wineskins and a large basket, which he handed to us, saying, "We bought these few things for you on the black market."

The things were fried sausages, the English type of sausage, bananas, tangerines, and long loaves of white bread. We toasted the sausages until they were burning hot and tasted faintly of wood smoke, and I do not think that I have ever eaten a more delicious meal by way of contrast to what had gone before. He also produced for the Americans long black cigarettes.

At 6 P.M. the guide led us out of the thicket and headed southwest, tearing across fields and on the beaten tracks around vineyards with his now familiar dancing, quick little steps, and heading for the silver line of a big river in the distance.

"How far are we going?" I asked.

"We shall be there in four hours at this pace."

Four hours! All of us had thought that we were going perhaps one mile, perhaps two.

"Ask him if there are many rivers to cross," said Charlie, for that was now our chief dread.

"Only two, but they are big ones."

The four hours slowly passed and we stopped in a hollow beside another stream, but this time we were not going to wade it. The guide's companion was going to his home by another route. Before he left, he embraced us warmly, insisted that we finish all the wine that remained in his skin, and then embraced us once again.

A few miles farther on, the guide tapped with a long stick on a farmhouse window. A light went on inside and then vanished. He tiptoed around to the front of the house, motioning to us that we must follow at his heels. When he had waited there for a few minutes to make sure that we were unobserved, he led us quickly through the front yard into a barn where there were two cows and a bull, through the barn to a stable occupied by a pony, a mule, and a draft horse, through the stable to a cellar filled with wine casks and demijohns, and thence up a spiraling stone staircase to a long living room, where several people were gathered around an open fireplace.

A thin, nondescript Spaniard came forward, said in French that he was from the British Consulate in Barcelona, and asked us to fill in our particulars, rank, regiment, et cetera, on a paper he carried.

The Catalan women took charge of us. They gave us warm water to wash with and cooked us a copious meal on the open fire.

The firelight sparkled in a decanter of red wine, a decanter with a narrow glass jet sticking out of its normal neck.

"All black market—a fine place this," the Spaniard from Barcelona remarked to me.

"Fine, fine," agreed our old guide testily. "But not so fine as my home, Englishman. Only I am outlawed. Here I am twelve kilo-

Crossing the Border

meters from my home, and not allowed by the government to sleep with my own buxom wife—I am an old man, but I believe in young wives; none of your scraggy old hens for me."

"Where are you going now, then?" For he had eaten a little, had drunk considerably, and was now dressing for the road.

"Where am I going? Why, home, of course. Nobody can prevent me from climbing in at my own bedroom window. And tomorrow I cross the mountains again. *Au revoir.*"

"An astonishing man," I said to the Spaniard from Barcelona.

"There are many astonishing men in Spain, but not many like him."

"He was divinely made," said one of the women. "He forgets that he is old, so he is as young as his grandsons."

They led us off to sleep in the hay. One of the sons forked down a lot of it; they spread blankets over this when we had flattened it out to make a big bed. All four of us lay down together; they put more blankets on top of us and more hay on top of that.

"You will sleep more comfortably tomorrow night, if all goes well," the Spaniard told us. "Try to sleep most of tomorrow. I shall return in the evening and we shall journey on together. We have to be very careful. I should warn you that the Spanish police are more clever than the Germans."

We slept until midday, when one of the squarely built farm women brought us a splendid golden-brown stew with mutton, beans, garlic, onion, and pimiento in it. There were beakers of a strange pinkish wine, strong and sweet.

Our new guide returned at five o'clock. He led us into the country for a few miles and then made us crouch beside him in a wood not far from what appeared to be a mixture between a grade crossing and a station. Perhaps in England it would have been called a "halt."

"That town is Figueras," he said, pointing to a glow of lights in the distance. "We are not going to board the train there. But if the police search the train and arrest you, then you must say that you boarded it at Figueras, and your tickets, which I now give to you, will bear out that statement. Is that understood?"

He waited while I translated.

"Next thing. We must not be seen by anybody outside the train while we board it at this station. We shall therefore leave this hiding place just before the train arrives. It will slow down well before the station and we shall jump in while it is moving. You will follow me into a long carriage like a Pullman car. You will separate, and will sit singly in opposite corners of the carriage. You will speak to nobody. I shall leave you in that carriage and sit in the carriage nearer the engine. The trip will take about two hours. When it is time to alight, I will walk back through the carriage. I will say nothing. I will not even look at you, but you must all individually get up and follow me. Is that understood?

"Now listen carefully. We must not be seen alighting from this train. You will follow me out onto the rear platform of the carriage. The last of you will shut the door behind him, and we shall all jump off while the train is moving. Be careful how you do this. We will drop off the right side of the train. Let your right foot gently down until it touches the ground, then run. We have no time for accidents. Is that understood?

"We will then find ourselves in a town. You will follow me at one-hundred-meter intervals, but staggered. That is to say that the man who follows me will be on the opposite pavement, and so on. When we pass the main hospital of the town we shall find a car waiting for us, a large black car. The car will allow us to pass, then will follow us to a piece of waste ground, where we shall all jump in. Is that clearly understood?"

"Oh, boy," said Charlie, when I had translated the last bit. "Does that car sound good!"

Although his plans had sounded a little fantastic to tired men, everything went exactly as he had predicted—until the bit about the car.

We passed the main hospital, we turned up a side street, we arrived at the piece of waste ground. But not a car was to be seen.

Crossing the Border

Our guide was so angry that he could scarcely speak intelligible French.

"There has been some accident. Wait here while I telephone for instructions. Remain standing against that wall, motionless and in absolute silence."

It was so cold out there in the moonlight that it was impossible to remain motionless without demanding frostbite. He had placed us against the wall because the moon was casting dark shadows. We stood there doing the cabman's exercise, and stamping our feet on the iron-hard ground.

Our position was made the more uncomfortable by contrast in that there was a large block of wide-windowed flats at the edge of our waste ground. Through the plate-glass windows we could see men and women sitting around, talking or reading or sewing or warming their buttocks by the dancing flames of large wood fires.

The guide's bad temper had not abated with his telephone conversation. All he would say was, "That creature has trains on the brain."

At length he calmed down sufficiently to tell me that our plans had been changed; we now had to jump a freight train.

"This is no easy matter. How many of you have jumped freight trains before? Have *you*?"

"No," I said.

"No," said Fritz.

"No," said Charlie.

"Yup," said the Trapper.

"Ah, one at least. That one must mount last of all. You, Englishman, since you have a bad leg, will mount first. Now, follow me."

He led us to the dark shade of a shelter in a cluster of tiny vegetable gardens. We were a few hundred yards outside a large marshaling yard and our shelter was fifty yards from the line. This guide was certainly an expert on trains. We waited for over an hour, and whenever a train pulled out of the marshaling yard he would peer at it in the moonlight.

"Confound it, not that one," he exclaimed. "These Spanish railways are really damnable. Always late, never on time, I earnestly assure you."

At last he shouted, "This is ours. Follow me closely."

He darted down to the railway, scaled the fence, and soon we were running with him alongside the train, which was picking up speed. I was carrying Charlie's parcel, and my first jump for the little iron ladder at the back of a truck failed because the weight of the parcels swung me around. At the second attempt all went well. The others followed me. The guide hung on to the ladder for a minute.

"Count the stations," he shrieked at us above the roar of the train. "Just before the *sixth* station, jump off. I shall remain on the truck behind this one." He vanished, climbing over the buffers.

Those Spanish freight trucks had tiny brake cabins stuck at the back, the roof of the cabin being raised some three feet above the roof of the truck. There was just room for the four of us to stand upright beside the heavy iron brake wheel. Any movement was out of the question. The top of the truck, stretching in front of us, was covered with a five-inch layer of gleaming white frost. There were no windows on the cab. As we stood squeezed there, like tinned asparagus in a refrigerator, little icicles formed on our hair and our eyelashes. The language in our cabin was terrible. When the train stopped at small stations, railwaymen would walk or run past us tapping at the wheels, unhooking a wagon behind, or shouting at somebody in the distance.

We saw the guide leap from the train like an elongated monkey, and scuttle off the track. We all did our best to emulate him, and followed him along a path that circled the sixth station and then rejoined the railway.

"We have a walk of three hours in front of us, going fast," the guide told us. "Most of it will be easy walking along the railway line."

By this time my leg appeared to have got accustomed to walk-

Crossing the Border

ing, but otherwise I knew that I had a chill and that no amount of fast walking could warm me.

We arrived in the early hours of the morning at a handsome farmhouse with shuttered windows and beautiful wrought-iron-work on balconies and gates. The guide found a key in the garden and opened the door of a garage containing, of all things, an Austin 7. From there he led us through a hall that held a lot of shining old furniture and a suit of armor, and then into a large kitchen.

A middle-aged couple came out in woolly dressing gowns to meet us. They lit a huge fire of brushwood and gave us coffee and white, home-baked bread with a lot of butter. The wife was pleased with me because she was French and I spoke her language.

"You have the red lights of fever in your cheeks and you must go to bed," she told me. She explained to the Americans in English with a powerful French accent: "The Englishman must have the single bed tonight because he is sick. You three will have to sleep in the double bed, but it is a very beeg one."

On the upstairs landing there was a portrait of General de Gaulle with the British, American, and French flags hanging above it. The bedroom was airy. French windows opened to a balcony with a view of moonlit hills and vineyards. There were linen sheets on my bed and colored blankets edged with silk.

The following morning they gave me some kind of drink, but nothing to eat. I slept most of the day, only half conscious that my American friends were being spirited away from me.

I was alone when I awoke at three o'clock and Madame gave me a treble brandy with warm milk.

"You will be well enough to eat dinner," Madame said. "Many of our young men arrive in your state. Sometimes we get the doctor and he says that it is a physical state, but I do not agree. He says it is a plain chill caught in the mountains and exaggerated by physical exhaustion. That is why it always passes quickly, he says, when the sick man has time to rest and sleep in a good bed.

"But I look at the young men who arrive like that, and I believe that the thing he calls a chill is a symptom of mental strain, nothing physical. It is because the young man has been wanting so much to cross the mountains, and for so long. He crosses them and something that was taut inside him suddenly sags. The doctor says it is a chill. But doctors are still groping in the dark. Now you are all right. I will bandage your bad leg (the doctor must see it in Barcelona), then you will put on your new clothes which you see laid out there, and you will come down and eat a solid meal with us. Just me and my son. My husband has gone to Barcelona with your friends. We like eating, my son and I."

While I memorized a plan of the route from Barcelona station to the British Consulate, Madame made a few quick alterations in my clothes. They were new clothes, Spanish ones, so that I should not arouse suspicions on the way to Barcelona. Then we ate.

We ate first a rice dish with mussels and oysters. Then for the three of us she brought in a platter with twelve large steaks upon it. Each of us ate four steaks, underdone, rubbed with garlic and pepper and salt, and cooked in butter. Then we had salad with dressing made from olive oil grown and pressed on the farm itself. I was surprised to find that I still wanted to sleep.

It was a small village station, and the passengers waiting on the unsheltered platform when I arrived early next morning were going to Barcelona for the day's work. It was still dark. Now I was respectably dressed (according to the standards prevailing locally) and they had given me a second-class ticket, since those were the least crowded carriages on that train.

The only thing that worried Madame about my appearance was my long, straw-colored hair, which stuck out in a kind of ruff over the back of my collar. I had not been able to have it cut properly since *le cocu* had taken me to the barber's shop near the cathedral in Strasbourg, three months earlier. It had been cut once at Les Daines by the tall railway policeman who had helped us to leave Annecy station. He had been a barber in civil life, and he claimed a barber's altitude record, for he had cut the hair of *maquisards* (Underground fighters) high up on Mont Blanc. But he had asked me, "I suppose you want *la coupe anglaise?*"

Crossing the Border

And when I replied in the affirmative, had shaped the hair around my ears but left the back uncut.

Long before my train arrived in Barcelona, my carriage was filled with suburbanites. Once again I was obliged to feign sleep in order to avoid being drawn into conversation.

I hurried through the station, well lighted and imposing, and crossed the town by memory from the plan Madame had made me memorize at the farm. They had told me that I would have no help on this walk unless I lost my way, but that I would be watched. And halfway to the Consulate I saw our train-jumping expert on the other side of the street. He stopped to light a cigarette, and cast one glint from his black eyes at me.

I found the Consulate without difficulty and, as instructed, walked quickly past the Spanish policeman, who sat in the hall, and up the staircase. At the top there was a man behind a desk, and rows of well-dressed townspeople waiting to make inquiries or to see people.

I gave my name to the man behind the desk.

"Just step along to that door marked Waiting Room, Mr. Millar."

A young Englishwoman came into the waiting room to find me.

"You are George Millar. We have been waiting for you for a long time."

I was almost home. . . .

. . . In Madrid, George Millar learned that the two Americans, Clark Gable and the Chauve-Souris, had reached Spain and were in Miranda prison. Soon he himself was sent to Gibraltar and so to England, where he heard that Wally Binns had been recaptured but had again escaped and was now in Switzerland.

Once home, George Millar volunteered for special service and after intensive training was parachuted back into France to work with the Maquis (Underground). For his wartime exploits he was decorated with the Distinguished Service Order and Military Cross and made Chevalier de la Légion d'Honneur with the Croix de Guerre avec Palmes.

6.

Escape from Hospital

Lieutenant Colonel Anthony Deane-Drummond, MC, is a professional soldier. In 1941, as a lieutenant, he was one of a picked team of paratroopers who were dropped in southern Italy to blow up an aqueduct. Their mission completed, they made for a rendezvous on the coast, where they were to be picked up by a British submarine. They were captured and sent to the prison camp at Sulmona.

Deane-Drummond made two attempts to escape from Sulmona and on the second managed to get via Milan as far as the Swiss border but was recaptured there. After serving thirty-five days in the cells as a punishment for this attempt he was sent to an escape-proof camp near Pisa.

Realizing the difficulty in escaping from this special camp, he faked illness and managed to get transferred to the military hospital in Florence. He took with him into hospital a navy-blue roll-neck pullover, battle-dress trousers with the outside pockets removed, brown shoes, and an Italian field service hat dyed chocolate brown. Although his room was on the top story of the hospital building, he determined to escape through the window. . . .

... When I was in my room, a *carabiniere* guard was on watch outside my door continuously, being relieved every eight hours. The door was kept locked. Every time I wanted to go to the lavatory I had to bang on it, when it was unlocked, and the *carabiniere* would walk with me to the lavatory just down the passage. When I sat on the veranda he came too, and the prospects of getting away did not seem very bright. Luckily the prison camp had not warned the hospital that I had escaped before and was considered "dangerous," or they would have taken rather more stringent precautions. Six months later in England I heard that the wretched commandant of the prison camp was sent to the Russian Front for not having warned the hospital! The dread the average Italian has for fighting for his country has always amused me. He would be prepared to go any length for a job at home, and being posted to an active front was always regarded as punishment. No wonder Italians were never much use as soldiers.

Outside my window was a seventy-foot drop to the courtyard below, and no handy drainpipes to slide down. The old device of knotted sheets for a rope could not be used because of the sheets' rottenness and the fact that the number I would require was many more than I could raise. However, there was a decorative molding about four feet below my window, which ran all the way around the outside of the building. The top of the molding was in the form of a slightly sloping ledge about five inches wide, and I thought it might be just wide enough to use.

Gradually my plan evolved. I would get out of my window and move along the ledge—past the Italian officer's bedroom window, around the corner of the building, and then in at one of the lavatory windows. I could easily make sure it was open by going to the lavatory about midnight. I would go through the lavatory door, which I would also leave open, and then down the stairs, which were in a well of their own and separated by doors from all landings. The snag was that I could not very well open the door leading down the stairs when I went to the lavatory, but I hoped that over a course of days I would be lucky one night and find that it had been left open. The *carabiniere* always sat in his chair facing my door, and he would be most unlikely to hear me flit in stockinged feet between the already opened lavatory and the stairway doors. Having reached the ground floor, I would jump out through a window into the courtyard, and circling around the building to the right, I could quite easily get onto the main road leading down into Florence.

I had been in the hospital a fortnight when my plan had crystallized. About then, a Flight Sergeant Cox came into my room for three days with tonsillitis. He was working as a batman at the Generals' Prison Camp at Fiesole, just outside Florence, having been captured when Air Vice-Marshal Boyd was landed by mistake in Sicily instead of Malta. He gave me all their news. He told me how Air Marshal Boyd spent his whole time doing carpentry, how General Gambier-Parry was a very able sketcher and artist, and how General Younghusband was a most successful gardener within the limited area that was available. General Carton de Wiart was the only one he could not understand, but "he has only one arm, one eye, and a Victoria Cross, so that must explain a lot." I agreed.

At the time I thought it was just possible that he was a stooge, and so I did not tell him of my intentions. It was a welcome respite, however, to be able to talk in English again.

As soon as Cox had gone back to Campo 12 at Fiesole, I started my midnight visits to the lavatory, but it wasn't until ten days later, on the evening of June 13, 1942, that the door leading down the stairway was left open. June 13 was St. Anthony's Day, which I felt was a good omen for my adventure.

I decided to start about 3 A.M. and aimed at being on the main road by 4 A.M. This would give me two hours to walk into Florence and get an early train to Milan. In planning for our escape from Campo 27, I had remembered that an express train for Milan was due to leave at 6 A.M., and that was the one I hoped to catch.

I dressed as silently as possible, putting one shoe in each trouser

Escape from Hospital

pocket, where they would not be in my way, and at 3 A.M., in my stockinged feet, I swung my legs over into the darkness and found the ledge with my toes. Holding on to the shutter outside the window with one hand, I started to move sideways to the left, flattening myself against the wall as much as possible. I had not gone more than a few steps when an attack of giddiness seized me, and I quickly went back, just managing to clutch on to my shutter again. My knees were shaking and my teeth chattering with excitement as I climbed back into my bedroom.

Ten minutes went by while I recovered my breath and my nerve. An occasional grunt came through the door from the *carabiniere*, or a squeak from his chair as he shifted his seat, but otherwise the night was silent. My imagination kept telling me that I might slip off the ledge, or it might crumble under my weight. But I knew I must do it. This was my chance; I might never get another one.

Once again I tiptoed to the window and, without looking down, levered myself out and slowly slithered my feet down the wall onto the ledge. This time I was not going to get back into the room; to make sure of it, I swung the outside shutters across the window, and I heard a click from the latch on the inside.

I had always meant to do this to keep the Italians guessing how I had got out, but on my first try I had forgotten all about it in my excitement. I had bought some particularly obnoxious and sticky hair oil while in the hospital, and I had used this to lubricate all the hinges and catches on the shutters and on the lavatory door, to stop any squeaks.

There was no going back now. I held on to the closed shutter with my right hand and slid as far as I could along the ledge. My left hand could not reach the shutter over the next window, but I forced myself on, and inch by inch moved along the ledge. I wanted to press against the rough wall as tightly as possible, but if I did this it would make a scraping noise that might alarm some wakeful patient.

After six feet with nothing to hang on to, I reached the next lot of shutters and, using them as handholds, quickly passed under the window. Then I came to the worst part of the ledge: where it went around the corner of the building, out of reach of all shutters. Again I had to let go with my right hand and move spread-eagled to the corner. Here the fingertips of my left hand were able to follow the wall around and give slightly more security. At the same moment, the ledge under my left foot suddenly felt loose, and I had visions of the whole corner of the building breaking away. All at once my giddiness returned, and I felt sweat slowly trickling down the side of my nose. My knees shook, but I held them still by pressing against the wall, while I gingerly transferred my weight to my other foot and felt around with my left toe to see what was loose. Something was very wobbly right on the corner, and looking down I could just see that the cement surface was quite free and, if dislodged, a three-foot length would crash into the courtyard below. The molding underneath the surface felt solid enough. It made a gritting noise as it wobbled and felt very insecure, but I slowly worked my way around the corner and then along a short length of wall to another corner, which was an inside one and much easier. A few more yards, and I was under the lavatory window.

I heaved myself up and dropped onto the lavatory floor, where I stood for a minute or two to get my breath. Never have I felt so relieved as I did when I had finished that awful traverse along the face of the building in the darkness. Never do I want to do anything like it again. It might have been child's play to an expert mountaineer, but I was not one.

Cautiously peering around the corner of the lavatory door, I saw the *carabiniere* awake and looking disconsolately at the ground in front of his chair. I saw that if I crossed the passage to the other side before moving along opposite the doorway to the stairs, he could not see me if he looked up. All went well, and soon I was at the doorway that led down the stairs. There was not enough room for me to get through and I prayed and hoped that it would not squeak when I opened it a further few inches. The door opened without a murmur, and like a flash I passed down the stairs, without the *carabiniere* knowing what was happening. I would have a clear five hours' start, till about 8 A.M., when I was called, and by that time I hoped to be well on the way to Milan. In case the *carabiniere* put his head inside my room during the remainder of the night, I had rolled up a greatcoat to look like me in bed, and I was confident it would pass all right for any casual look.

When I had crept down the stairs, I dropped into the courtyard through an open window on the ground floor. I had rather misjudged the height, because I landed on the paving stones on all fours and severely strained my wrist in the process. I crept around the outside of the hospital and then through an empty lot, and so came to the wall bordering the main road, where I put on my shoes. I also pulled out a brown paper parcel from my trouser pocket, which I planned to carry instead of a bag to give me the necessary *raison d'être*. It was five minutes to four, and at four o'clock precisely I swung over the wall and started to walk down the main road toward Florence.

This time I had decided to wear no outer insignia, to suggest that I was a German. I did not, in fact, have any papers with me, as it would have been too risky to bring them into the hospital. Only if I was challenged would I say I was a German, and then only if I had to say more than a word or two in Italian. By 5 A.M. I had reached the center of Florence and had to ask my way to the station, which I reached about twenty minutes later. To my relief I found that there was a 6 A.M. train to Milan, but I decided to wander around the station till about ten minutes to six before buying my ticket. By that time there would be a good-sized line, and this would give the booking clerk less time to look at me closely.

The Florence station is modern, and puts ours to shame by its cleanliness and neat layout. I looked around for a bench, where I feigned sleep to avoid complications in talking. When the time came, I pulled out my money and rose to join the line for tickets. Unfortunately, my 500-lire note was slightly mutilated because it had been hidden up the tubular leg of an iron bedstead at Campo 27 and little holes had been torn in it. Eventually my turn came and I said, "*Terzo Milano,*" at the same time pushing over the note. To my horror, the official started turning the note over and over, examining it against the light, and, after what seemed hours, asked me if I had another. I replied with a shake of the head and a monosyllabic mumbled "no." However, with a shrug of his shoulders, he pushed the ticket and change toward me. Cold sweat had started on my brow, and the palms of my hands were decidedly damp as I walked away.

The express from Rome came in ten minutes late, and was very full. As soon as it came to a halt, the crowd surged forward, I included, and we fought for places on the steps leading up to the carriages. Putting my head down, I got aboard, after giving a kick on the shins to a man on my left who had tried to pull me back to get in himself. At last we all crammed into the corridor, where I stood in the corner near the lavatory, chin on chest, pretending to doze. I kept my ticket in my hand, and whenever the collector passed up and down the train, which happened frequently, he just took the ticket out of my hand, punched it, and put it back without apparently waking me up.

A lot of people got out at Bologna, and I was glad to find a seat to myself in a compartment, as I would need all my energy when I reached the frontier. Unfortunately, no *cistina* (basket) lunches were being sold on the stations, rations in Italy being much shorter now than when I had traveled to Milan six months earlier.

On one occasion when the ticket collector came around, he had two railway police behind him, and they took a good look at me when he punched the ticket. He took the ticket out into the corridor and started examining it closely, with his back to me. After a minute or two, he returned it and passed on to the next person. Scare over! Apparently they had a special key that fitted the ticket exactly for detecting forgeries. In all my travels on the railway I always saw hundreds of *carabiniere,* railway policemen, and ordinary railway officials, but they were always more con-

Escape from Hospital

cerned with the traveler who had no ticket. As long as you had a bonafide ticket, they did not seem to worry.

I managed to avoid all conversation by pretending to sleep in my corner, and at 11 A.M. we pulled into Milan Central Station. My plan was to hang about the station till about 4:30 P.M. and then take a train to Varese, as I thought Como might be watched by now. The frontier was only thirteen kilometers from Varese at Porto Ceresio on the edge of Lake Lugano. If I arrived at Varese about dusk, I would walk to within two kilometers of Porto Ceresio and then strike up the hill, and with a bit of luck might be in Switzerland within twenty-four hours of getting away from Florence.

The waiting room was much emptier this time, and I killed time by wandering around the station. I bought my ticket, just in case anybody asked me what I was doing, and got a return this time to make traveling to a frontier town more plausible. "*Terzo Varese andate e ritorno*," accompanied by a 50-lire note, produced my ticket without any questions being asked. I was always a little self-conscious about my dress, but it never seemed to excite any suspicions. Luckily it was fairly cool at that date, and the roll-neck pullover did not look too much out of place.

I had a cup of *caffè al latte* for my lunch and, buying a few papers, took them to the waiting room for a four-hour wait till my train, which left at 4:37 P.M. I saw in the paper that a German ship had been sunk in the Mediterranean and the survivors had landed at Genoa. This might be a useful story if I was stopped, and my navy-blue sweater would help. I could always pretend I was taking a short holiday before going on to Germany.

The journey to Varese by electric train was without incident, and I arrived at about 6:15 P.M., just when it was beginning to get dark. My half ticket was taken without any questions being asked, and I went out into the town. My plan was to strike off along the road that led roughly in the right direction, and I hoped it would bring me to a signpost that would put me on my way. I walked right through the center of the town and past groups of men and women gossiping on the pavements and sitting at open-air cafés; but they seemed to be far more interested in their own conversations than in me, so I passed through unmolested.

A crossroad on the north side of the town put me on the right road and told me I had twelve kilometers to Porto Ceresio. By this time it was dark and the sky overcast, but a moon shone behind the clouds for the first half of the night. The road twisted and turned in all directions but always seemed to be flanked by small fields, high walls, or precipitous mountainsides. It was no country to choose one's own route until much closer to the frontier. The road seemed to be interminable. My month in the hospital without exercise had not helped, and my muscles were very soft. I passed through one or two tiny villages and eventually came to the three-kilometer stone from Porto Ceresio, where I could see Lago Lugano with its searchlights playing on the water. By this time it was 10 P.M., and I struck up the hillside through a wood which flanked the road at this point. Thornbushes seemed to reach out and grab me with every step I took and made progress very slow and painful. It was dark in the wood, and I was forced to move so slowly that, having gone about two hundred yards, I decided to wait until morning, when I would be able to avoid some of the worst hazards. Feeling thirsty, tired, and cold, I curled myself up in some dead leaves and went to sleep. The cold woke me up about an hour before dawn, and after rubbing my stiff muscles back to life, I crawled up the hill, trying to avoid the demon thornbushes. After half an hour, I saw I was coming to the top of the ridge. Suddenly, outlined against the morning sky, I saw a sentry box with a tall row of barbed wire behind it. I immediately dropped to the ground and saw that the sentry boxes were spaced about fifty yards apart all along the top of the hill. Just around the corner, and lower down, I could see what looked like a cemetery. This was really too much! My map did not show the frontier in any great detail, but I had never expected to find it so close to the main road and so well guarded. In a minor panic I slithered back down the hill up which I had just crawled, and wondered what to do next. I was really flabbergasted, having

Escape from Hospital

hoped that this piece of the frontier would not have been more difficult than the part near Chiasso that I had seen six months before. Rightly or wrongly I decided to lie up where I was for the rest of that day, and then to walk back to Varese and on to Como that night. I would then try to get over a piece of frontier that I knew.

Later on, in Switzerland, I found a large-scale map of where I had been, and the frontier could not have been there at all and was at least another two kilometers farther on. To this day I do not know what I had stumbled into, and can only suppose that it was some kind of military dump that was being guarded extra well. I had not bargained for that sort of bad luck. To make matters worse, it rained cats and dogs all that day, and I was soaked to the skin. I had to remain perfectly still so as not to attract attention, and I don't think I have ever been so cold in all my life. My teeth kept up a permanent chatter and the feeling went out of my hands and feet after an hour or two. Slowly the time went by and at last it was dark enough to allow me to walk down to the main road and get my circulation going once more. It was about twenty miles to Como, and I thought I could arrive in its vicinity by midnight.

It was lovely to be warm again and my clothes soon dried out, but I was certainly not out of the woods yet. I passed through Varese for the second time about 9 P.M., and found the Como road without difficulty. I began to feel extraordinarily tired, and my brown Italian shoes were working up beautiful blisters on my heels, which did not help progress. To my left I could see the outline of hills and over them I knew lay Switzerland, my dream country for over a year past. The road seemed never ending, and I began to curse myself for having decided to walk all the way around to Como before trying again. If I had had a more accurate map of the frontier, I would have gone across country, but it was too risky on my own and would have been more guesswork than map reading.

I don't know what possessed me, but I went on walking after

midnight, always a dangerous thing to do. At about 1 A.M., while passing through the little village of Ogliate, I was challenged. My spirits fell as I went up to the man who proved to be a *maresciallo* (a master sergeant) of the Bersaglieri. He asked me for my papers. I went into a long explanation of who I was and brought out my newspaper to prove it, but all I could get out of him was that I would have to go *"dentro"* (inside) for the night. The last card I had to play was to knock him on the head, seize his bicycle, and make a run for it, but before this I tried my last piece of bluff. I told him that if the German consular authorities in Como did not see me by eight in the morning, there would be trouble for anyone who had held me. I said this with much gusto and repeated myself several times. With much head-shaking and more muttering of *"dentro,"* he said I could go on this time, but it was most irregular and I must not do it again. My luck was holding out, but that scare had brought me to my senses, and I did not make such a stupid mistake again. I went on through the village and slept in a ditch about one kilometer along the road till about 4:30, when I started to walk again. I passed through another village and had a dirty look from *carabiniere* on duty, but soon after this I discovered a little wood near the road that would do as shelter for the day. Creeping in under some undergrowth, I curled up and went to sleep, mentally and physically exhausted but thankful that I was still a free man.

 I woke up at 11 A.M. to the sound of woodcutting and children playing about a hundred and fifty yards away in my wood. Children and dogs were my worst enemies that day, but luckily none came near enough to find me, though this had the effect of keeping me mentally alert and awake all the time. I was now getting very hungry and thirsty, and my blistered feet did not help my physical condition. However, I knew that I was now within a few miles of freedom and that, given a bit of luck and provided I did not make a fool of myself, I would have a good chance of succeeding. It was my gamble against at least another six months in prison, if not for the whole war. I was playing for uncomfortably high stakes. I suppose the chances of getting out of a

Escape from Hospital

prison camp are at least a hundred-to-one against. In Italy at this time, one's chances of getting to the frontier area, once having got out of camp, were about twenty-to-one against—provided one did not do anything too stupid. Having got to within five miles of the frontier, the chances of getting over would be about even. I had now, for the second time in six months, arrived within five miles of the frontier, so I considered my chances really good, but I did not mean to take any risks.

That day, thank goodness, was dry; for I don't think I could have stood another soaking. When dusk came, I started on what I hoped would be my last lap. The road began to climb and, in a series of gentle turns, I went on upward for the first three hours. The country was getting very hilly, and the mountains to the north seemed to tower to endless heights above me. An occasional car swept by and I would shield my face from the lights and try to keep in the shadows on the sides of the road. Houses either side became more frequent. They were obviously summer villas for rich businessmen from Milan, and must have been delightful, with an endless view stretching out over the Lombardy plain.

A few men passed me going the other way, and once two or three soldiers went by, but they had no eyes for me and I certainly had none for them. At last my road started to wend its way down the hillside and, far below, I could see some lights with a lake beyond. At the time I assumed this must be Como, but I discovered later that it was the goods yard at Chiasso, on the frontier, at which I was now looking.

Eventually, at about 11 P.M., I came to a road junction and turned left toward the lights, thinking that it would lead me to Como, through which I would have to pass before reaching the frontier area at Chiasso. In fact, of course, my road had bypassed Como, and I had just joined the Como–Chiasso road, where I had been caught before. I suppose I should have recognized it, but it looked very different by night, and distances were deceptive.

I walked on down the hill to Chiasso and did not realize my mistake until suddenly I saw the frontier barrier right across the road, not two hundred yards away from me. I nearly had a fit on the spot. Trying not to hurry myself, I retraced my steps to the outskirts of Chiasso, and not wishing to be caught on the road again after hours, I decided to sleep in a culvert under the road until about 4:30 A.M., when I would go back toward Como for about a mile and then strike up the hill. My culvert could not have been more than a few hundred yards from the frontier, but it was a case of "safety first" at this stage. Unfortunately, the culvert was not entirely dry, and an evil-smelling stream of dirty black water trickled down the middle. I had an uncomfortable, worrying five hours perched on some flat stones that remained dry at one side of the stream.

At last 4:30 A.M. crept around on my watch, and making sure that nobody saw me coming out of the culvert, I started walking back down the road. In ten minutes I found a convenient turning-off point and soon I was following a small footpath that led up the hillside and approximately in the right general direction. I would be much too early for any woodcutters going to work, and my only worry was the possibility of frontier guards coming back from duty along my track. However, I reasoned to myself that the relief guard would surely have to use my track to go out, and I could not imagine a change-over much before 6:30 A.M. With any luck, my path would be all right for at least an hour, and after that I must keep well clear of all tracks. My progress along the path was five times as quick as it would have been across country, as by now I was climbing nearly vertical slopes with thick thorny undergrowth on either side.

At 6 A.M. I decided to leave the track and started climbing straight up the hill. I was now about two thousand feet above the valley. I could see Chiasso quite plainly with its long goods sidings, and an obvious fence at right angles through the middle—the frontier.

I decided to climb for about another hour, and then to start moving very slowly along the hillside till I sighted the frontier. I would then lie up all day watching the sentries, and try to get over that night.

I thrust my way up the mountainside and swept aside the

bushes that tried to hold me back; what did a few scratches matter now? Soon I came to a belt of pine trees, and walking through them was a great relief after the thorn-scrub lower down. I came out of the pine trees and went on upward through hazel plantations and every sort of mountain shrub, which all grew in profusion everywhere. At last I thought I was high enough and started to move cautiously along the hillside in the direction where I knew the frontier to be. I had not been going for more than half an hour when, just across a little valley and not more than four hundred yards away, I saw a sentry box among the trees. I dropped down on one knee and could pick out one of two more and the line of fence poles behind. The little valley between me and the frontier was quite bare and open, and the fence and sentry boxes were a few yards inside the wood beyond. I found a comfortable hole full of dead leaves in which I could sleep and from which I could watch the frontier. I had a very welcome meal of blueberries, which grew all around; and after watching the frontier for an hour or two, fell asleep.

About half a mile up on my left hand, and just about where the frontier ought to be, I could see a red roof. I assumed this to be one of the posts that housed the relief sentries, and occasionally I could see one wandering along the wire. They changed over every even hour. The sentry boxes were about two hundred yards apart, which was not too bad, and I carefully marked down the route I should take that night in order to bring me out exactly between two boxes.

At last darkness fell, and although I felt like going bald-headed at it, I had decided to play safe and try to cross at 11 P.M. I would allow an hour to crawl the four hundred yards, and that would give me at least another hour before there was any more large movement of sentries to and fro. The sentries on that frontier were not overly keen on wandering about by day; so, with any luck, they would be even less alert at night. A light rain started to fall about 10 P.M., and I cheered inwardly to myself. No Italian sentry would wander about in the rain unless given a direct order by an officer!

I crawled slowly though the undergrowth and across the open patch at the bottom of the valley. I did not make much noise, but to my ears I sounded like a bull charging around. The rain pattering on the leaves made all the difference, as it blanketed my sounds from the sentries. I could just hear one singing away to himself in his box, little suspecting that a British officer was at that very moment within a hundred yards of his post.

By 11 P.M. I had reached the path used by the sentries, and just over the other side the frontier wire was stretched. I saw that it was a fairly formidable obstacle. Made of diamond mesh wire of fairly heavy gauge, it was constructed all in one piece, and at least twelve feet high. Poles in the form of an inverted V suspended the wire, and bells were hung all along the top. The slightest touch on the wire would start them clanging. The problem was how to get over, through, or under. No branches overhung the wire anywhere near, and as I had no pliers, my only alternative was to try to burrow a way underneath. I could have risked the bells and climbed over the top, but it might have gone wrong and was not worth it if I could find another way.

The bottom of the fence was pegged every six inches with eighteen-inch wooden stakes, but luckily the soil in which the wood was set was mostly leaf mold, and the stakes pulled up easily without shaking the fence. I had soon freed about a three-foot length, pausing between each stake to listen for any footsteps on the path.

All was quiet. The sentry on my left was still crooning away to himself about his *"Mamma mia,"* but I could hear nothing from the one on my right. The rain came down a little harder now, and a damp, moist smell came up from the disturbed earth when I started to scrape it away with my hands. It reminded me of sheltering from the rain in an English wood in autumn after a dry summer. It was a musty clean smell quite different from the usual pungent Italian aromas.

I slowly scraped away, using one of the stakes to loosen the earth, and then removing it with my hands.

Escape from Hospital

After I had been going about ten minutes there was quite a respectable hole, and I tried to squeeze underneath the wire; but there was too small a gap and I became stuck with one shoulder and one arm in Switzerland and the rest of me in Italy.

Several things then happened at once. The bell above me gave a very small tinkle, a branch crashed down nearby, the sentry stopped singing, and the noise of shunting goods wagons in Chiasso suddenly became very loud due to a change in the wind.

I prayed that the sentries would stay where they were, while I slowly pushed myself back into Italy. The hole would have to be bigger.

After a few very long seconds I was clear, and I crawled back over the track and lay in a bush for a few minutes. If the sentry had heard anything, he would surely come along and inspect the wire at once.

My luck was in and after five minutes' complete silence, except for the rain on the leaves, and the noise of the shunting, I crawled back across the track once more. On this occasion I was not going to be stuck under the wire, and I worked away for ten minutes before the gap was big enough. My hands reached through to Switzerland, this time much farther, and I was able to grasp a tree root and draw myself through without shaking the fence above me. . . .

. . . Anthony Deane-Drummond reached the British Embassy in Berne, and arrangements were made for him to be passed along an escape line through France to the Mediterranean. He was picked up by the Royal Navy at a spot some fifty miles west of Marseilles and landed in Gibraltar. Ten days later he was in Scotland.

This was not Deane-Drummond's last escape. He was dropped by parachute into the famous Battle of Arnhem, and made prisoner again. He escaped after hiding for thirteen days standing upright in a cupboard in a German guardroom. With the help of Dutch patriots, he regained the British lines.

7.

The Land of You-Never-Know

Lieutenant W. B. Thomas, a New Zealander, was badly wounded and captured by the Germans in their invasion of Crete. His captors flew him to the mainland of Greece, where he was taken to a military hospital.

Although there was a gaping wound in his thigh, Lieutenant Thomas dreamed of escape; but it was nearly four months before he could get out of bed.

His first escape from the hospital, with his leg still not healed, was a gallant wire-cutting attempt under fire from the guard. Both he and his companion got away but were soon recaptured.

Thomas's next idea was to feign death and be carried out of the hospital in his coffin. This plan might well have succeeded, but the German doctor, with whom Thomas had become friendly, came to take one last look at his prisoner-patient. When the sheet covering his face was reverently drawn down, the "dead" man giggled—and the game was up.

The final attempt to escape from the hospital was the signal for *his guards to send him to a permanent prisoner-of-war camp in Germany. It was from the transit camp in the port of Salonika that the following successful escape was made....*

. . . Soon after midday on October 30, with snow-capped Olympus on our left, we steamed up the Gulf of Salonika to tie up in that historic port.

Above the harbor, the old stone city walls, the towers and the fortresses standing out on the hill gave a medieval atmosphere, but around the docks things were modern enough. There was a small amount of German and Italian shipping about, with here and there a cruiser or a destroyer from Mussolini's fleet. German Marines, none of whom seemed more than eighteen years old, paraded on the wharves, constantly saluting their smart-looking officers. Everybody seemed busy, but all were very interested in the Englanders as we were off-loaded and shepherded into Red Cross vans. We were driven along the waterfront, past the great circular tower of Salonika, and in a few minutes were at the gates of the prison camp.

My heart sank at the sight. Here was no hospital wire. This was a real prison camp. High mazes of barbed wire ran at all angles. Throughout the camp were great towers on which sentries could be seen fondling their machine guns. From behind the wire near the gate, a crowd of unkempt and undernourished prisoners gathered to gape forlornly as we were formed into ranks and our luggage was checked.

It was almost dark by the time all our personal belongings had been strewn on the gravel and the Guard Officer was satisfied that we carried no implements for escape. The great gates opened and we poured in, to be ushered into various buildings.

In a large dormitory I met again quite a few of the officers who had come up from Athens in the hospital ship. We all fell to exchanging experiences, and I felt quite at home among them. Two in particular I came to respect immensely. Lieutenant Colonel Le Soeuf, tall, dark, and quiet-spoken, had been captured with his unit, the Seventh Australian Field Ambulance, when they were overrun at Heraklion in Crete; Maj. Richard Burnett, a regular officer, had been commanding officer of his unit on Crete and was captured while making a reconnaissance in the dark.

Salonika was a bad camp in every way. In the past, many shocking atrocities had been committed by guards who had been former members of the Nazi Youth Movement. Burnett was even then investigating a horrible case—a German sentry had thrown a grenade into a latrine packed with dysentery cases and the carnage had been frightful. The only explanation given on Burnett's protest was that the men were whispering in a suspicious manner. The authorities supported the sentry's action.

In a recent unsuccessful attempt at escape, three men had been shot out of hand and their bodies left for days in the hot sun, while four other escaped soldiers had been bound with barbed wire and whipped as a warning to all. Drunken guards had been known to walk into the compound and cruelly maul unarmed prisoners, and it was said that the officer in charge of the young Nazis would ask daily of his guard how many English swine had been killed, and congratulate the murderer effusively.

It was an alarming picture, quite different from the treatment I had experienced in Athens. Listening to it all, I regretted very much that I had ever left the hospital.

The camp had been an old Greek artillery barracks, but the Germans had allowed it to deteriorate badly, so that now it was in a terrible state of sanitation, with practically no drainage at all. Millions of flies swarmed around the latrines and cookhouses and formed ugly black heaps where refuse was dropped. Scores of mangy cats slunk among the barrack rooms.

The prisoners in the compound were the stragglers of the large army that had already passed through to Germany. There were thirty officers and some two hundred men, one hundred and fifty of whom were maimed in some way.

About fifteen were men who had lately been caught in and

The Land of You-Never-Know

around Salonika. These were a grand crowd of fellows, and I made a point of talking to them and so gained much valuable information.

Some had been out and recaptured four or five times; indeed, the greatest joke among them was the case of the Australian who was picked up as a matter of course by a German patrol each Friday at a house of ill fame. Others with higher motives for escape had been free for long periods, only to be recaptured either on the very borders of Turkey or at sea moving south to freedom.

One, a tall New Zealand sergeant with a sense of humor, had seen his chance on a day of pouring rain, when a German officer had visited the camp hospital. The officer had walked into the lobby and hung up his dripping coat and hat before entering the German guardroom. The sergeant had donned these quickly and marched out into the rain. The sentries had all, one by one, frozen into a salute. Thereafter, he walked down into the streets of Salonika. It was truly an escape to fire the imagination.

A long-haired lad from Sussex had clung to the bottom of one of the contractor's drays and had been carried out of the camp. A very young Cockney told us of his adventure in going out in a bag of rubbish.

The prisoners were even then working on a mass escape plan. But they had the shrewdness of experienced escapists. It was some days before I was to be allowed into their confidence.

Meanwhile, the atmosphere in the officers' mess was unpleasantly strained. There were bickerings over food all around, and quarrels between the Medical Corps and the combatants over such futile things as seniority and the post of Senior British Officer in Captivity. On one occasion feeling ran so high that one side actually asked a German NCO to consider and settle the dispute.

It was not a pleasant place. Consequently I was pleased when Dick Burnett asked me to share a room accorded him because of his rank.

Burnett was keen on escape. He had been free on more than one occasion in Crete, and in spite of his forty years was determined to risk all the hazards to get back to his regiment. For as long as he was to be a prisoner, he was firmly resolved to cause as much trouble for his captors as possible.

For the first three or four days, I think, he was weighing me up as a possible partner for the months we might have to spend together before reaching British lines.

Then we began to lay our plans.

The section of the camp we were concerned with was only a small part, a subsection, of the main Salonika Prison Camp. Most of the other subsections were now empty and unguarded, with the exception of the one immediately to the west of ours. This held political prisoners from Greece and Yugoslavia. In there we had one day seen an old lady awaiting execution for aiding British escapers.

The subsection was an oblong, some three hundred yards by two hundred, containing seven large barrack huts, a cookhouse, and a large new building. The only exit was the gate at the northwest corner, and apart from the roving sentries within the compound, the Germans relied mainly on the guard posts immediately outside it. At the southern end, these consisted of two twenty-foot towers, each with two sentries, a machine gun, and a movable searchlight. At the northern end, there were the sentries on the gate, those on a tower by the gate, and two sentries with machine gun and searchlight on the roof of a small shed used for storing horse fodder. The south and west sides were bounded by other subsections, the north by an open space and the Salonika road, and the east side had a wide gravel road that separated the compound from rubbish and salvage, and which led along to the stables.

A whole morning spent watching guards, drawing innumerable diagrams, and getting annoyed with one another disposed of the front, the west, and rear sides as quite impossible. Only the east side was left, and we had little hope that it would produce the answer. In common with the others, it had some three hundred yards of wire tangle, ten feet high, ten feet wide, but there was one difference. There were two buildings that broke the obstacle, that is, the wire tangle ran between them and rambled up and over them. It did not run along the back.

One of these was the cookhouse. It had a thick cement wall for a back and furthermore was less than a stone's throw from the southern sentry tower. We mooched around it for half an hour after lunch and rejected it as impracticable.

The second house, the medical building, was a fairly new three-storied structure. A preliminary examination revealed no possibilities; all the windows facing out were heavily barred with steel and barbed wire, even if work could free them, it would be too dangerous to be lowered to the road below in full view of the searchlights at either end.

But just as we were deciding dejectedly that a tunnel was the only solution, we espied a staircase winding down from the ground floor to hide what must be a back doorway onto the gravel road below. The passage down was blocked by large empty crates. The door was of itself unimportant. There were still the searchlights and machine guns covering the road outside. But Dick had an idea and we climbed back onto the first floor to discuss it.

The two searchlights that concerned us covered the road very efficiently. The one at the south end from the tower had an unobstructed view, while the one on the roof of the hay shed was only limited by its position from seeing the actual back of the building in question. But, and on this our plan depended, these posts had the additional task of covering the south and north wire respectively: their searchlights were on swivels, and they would swing from one task to the other every few seconds. For the most part, one or other of the posts would have its light focused on the gravel road; occasionally both would play together along it for minutes on end. But with an understandable human error, often for a few seconds, both crews would switch simultaneously onto their secondary task. This would leave the road in darkness until either of them realized the position and swung his searchlight back. Burnett and I considered that, given luck, these erratic few seconds would give us a chance to make the initial dash across the road and use the scant cover of a shallow culvert before the searchlights swung back.

And so we examined the door.

The crates barring the steps down from the first floor were really no obstacle and would afford good cover for any work we should do. The steps ran down in two short flights onto a very small landing, and the doorframe was set firmly in stone. There were steel and wooden bars across it, both bolted and nailed, and the whole was covered with barbed wire on staples. Formidable certainly, but, provided we were not hurried, we thought it could be done.

One remarkable thing about our work on this project was the complete absence of the adventure spirit and the elation of imaginary success. Every step we took in this venture was coldly methodical. We took very few into our confidence.

Amazingly enough, the tools for the work were no trouble at all. I bought a pair of excellent pliers from a Greek electrician working in the barracks; Burnett made some useful crowbars from sections of our beds; and Fred Moodie, a camp doctor, provided a pair of strong plaster cutters. Fred also arranged for me a good supply of the German cod-liver-oil salve which had proved very soothing and beneficial to my wound.

We started work that night. Immediately after the evening check we made our way to the building with innocent unconcern and talked to various orderlies until curfew, when we slipped behind the crates under the first flight of stairs until all was quiet.

The work was necessarily slow, and not a little nerve-racking. Each nail, each bolt had to be worked out slowly and with great caution; a loud squeak would leave us perspiring and fearful for long minutes. Every now and then the crunch of heavy feet on the gravel outside would hold us up, and on three occasions during

The Land of You-Never-Know

the first night, two of the guard talked for a long time just outside the door.

By four o'clock we had removed all the wooden bars and two of the six more formidable steel bars. We tacked the bars back loosely into their old position and generally tidied up the evidence before setting off on the quite hazardous trip back to our barracks. The two sentries detailed to prowl around inside the compound had orders to shoot on sight after curfew, and though the twenty minutes they took on their regular rounds provided ample time for us, there were the searchlights to pin us down occasionally and always the chance that the sentries might vary their tactics.

We reached our room without incident and were sound asleep for the six-o'clock room check. Having previously convinced the Germans that it was less trouble not to order us out to stand by our beds each morning (as laid down), we were left to slumber on until almost lunch time.

Our progress on the second night did not compare with the first night. There were too many interruptions—stable hands coming home late from leave and arguing out on the road, restless sentries, and irregular changing of guards. And we were discovered at work by a group of Australian and British medical orderlies, and it took us some little time to impress on them the need for absolute secrecy. However, we worked out two more steel bars and managed to loosen a third before an early rooster, crowing beyond the stables, warned us of approaching day.

On the third night we made very good progress indeed; by eleven o'clock the last of the steel bars was disposed of. We had brought a rough chisel and a screwdriver to remove the lock, but, to our amazement, we found that it was not, in fact, locked. A few nails had been hammered at random around the edges, however, and just after midnight the last was worked out and we were able to move the door.

It opened two or three inches and then stuck. We realized that there was an apron of barbed wire stapled on to the outside. With some difficulty it would be possible to worm a wrist with pliers through the opening. After a short consultation we decided to leave it as it was until the night of the break, knowing that it would only take a few minutes to open it.

We made our way carefully back to our room, secreted our tools under our mattresses and in the stove, and undressed in the dark. It was only about one o'clock, and tired as we were, the prospect of a few extra hours' sleep was very pleasing.

No sooner had we said good-night, however, than we were suddenly startled by the tread of heavy feet in the passageway outside. There was a guttural order, our door burst open, and three soldiers rushed in. Torches flashed in our faces, our blankets were pulled off roughly, and the room was quickly but not thoroughly searched. Then, as if satisfied, the officer barked an order, and the party clattered out and away, leaving two very shaken men behind.

Now that visit was unfortunate. The explanation was quite beyond us, particularly as ours was the only room searched. Perhaps someone had discovered and reported that we had not been sleeping in our beds at night; or perhaps it was merely a check on me as a known "bad lad." But the effect was this: Burnett decided not to come. Three nights' work had taxed his nerves badly, and now he thought our whole plan was discovered. Even when daylight proved that no attempt was made to refix the door, Burnett saw the possibility of a trap—a machine gun covering the exit to make an example of anyone who attempted to escape. He was still as determined as ever, but with the caution of forty years he weighed the chances as too dangerous, and started straight away on a new plan—to throw ourselves from the train on the way through Yugoslavia.

His pessimism shook me not a little. I spent the morning watching the area near the cookhouse, and after lunch sat down and tried to come to some decision. His arguments were very sound; the plan had been hazardous enough without the new threat. Yet at the back of my mind was a conviction, however unfounded, that the plan was still secret.

The Land of You-Never-Know

Finally I took out a piece of paper, and ruling a line down the center, wrote in two columns all the pros and cons I could think of.

That was a poignant half hour. I knew well that the wrong decision might cost me my life. Yet I felt very strongly that it was a case of now or never, that, if I let this opportunity pass, I might never be presented with another.

As the page filled up, Burnett sat quietly watching me. I knew that he was apprehensive, but, having stated his arguments once, he made no attempt to dissuade me further.

Before I could make up my mind, we were besieged by some five or six of the more hardened card players and I was quite willing to procrastinate an hour for a game of pontoon. Perhaps it was my abstraction, but within half an hour, without effort, I had taken every drachma off the whole school. After a drink of cocoa from my Red Cross parcel they all departed very disgruntled, threatening that they would come back on the morrow to get it all back. As soon as they had gone, at Burnett's suggestion, I entered under the "Pros" that fact that I now had eight thousand drachmas for escape purposes.

At six o'clock I made my decision. It was, I am sure, the decision of my life. Our original plan had been to get some greatly needed rest that night, Saturday, and to escape on Sunday about nine, when the guards not on duty were on leave. But now, as things appeared to be moving rapidly and my nerves were so tense that I could not sleep, I decided to go on my own that night.

When Burnett saw that I was determined, he gave me everything he had: all his bread, his condensed Red Cross food, a civilian coat, and all his savings, including some English money. He cooked me up a wonderful farewell meal and set himself to do a thousand and one little things to help me to get ready.

It was now after curfew. It was therefore necessary to move with great care over to the building. Soon after eight thirty, I said good-bye to Burnett. He was terribly apprehensive of the risk

I was taking and heartily miserable that he was not coming with me. I realized I was going to miss his company very much.

It took me almost an hour to go the two hundred yards from our barracks. The searchlights seemed particularly restless, and the roving patrol sat down and talked for nearly half an hour while I lay in what shade a wire-netting fence afforded. When finally they moved off, I ran quickly up the steps and through the door into the hall of the medical building. As soon as I latched the door behind me, a startled voice greeted me.

"Are you *mad?* Surely you know that it's dangerous to be out at curfew?"

It was an Australian medical orderly. When I told him of my plans, he immediately offered his help.

We moved onto the first landing, from where we could look through the barred window down onto the road. Everything seemed quite normal. We watched for half an hour, but, with the exception of a team of horses being taken out from the stables, only the usual movement was apparent.

The orderly and a friend appointed themselves to keep watch while I worked. We arranged a code of signals whereby, should they wish to warn me, they would throw something small down the steps leading to the escape door. The "all clear" would be one or the other whistling from *Rigoletto.*

The door was as we had left it. I removed all the loosely held bars and convinced myself that no one had tampered with them. The door opened noiselessly some three inches, and even with great caution it only took me twenty minutes to cut the eight or nine restraining wires on the outside.

As I cut the last one and felt the door suddenly swing easily toward me, the first alarm signal in the form of a leather slipper clattered down the stairs behind me. I closed the door quickly, my heart in my mouth. Outside I could hear heavy feet crunching slowly down the road. As they approached the door, I held my breath in apprehension. With the searchlights full on, I felt that no one could miss the telltale loose ends of wire. But, although I could have sworn there was a slight pause just level with the door, the danger passed, and in a few seconds I heard a soft but unmusical attempt to whistle the arranged all clear.

I opened the door a few inches and studied the ground. The road was only some fifteen feet across, but I realized that unless the searchlights settled down, I would never get over without being seen. The sentry in the tower on the south end was unusually restless; his light was flickering to and fro every few seconds. I decided, as it was then nine thirty, to wait until the ten-o'clock change of sentries, with the hope of getting someone more placid. During the wait I worked out each step across the road, and the point where I should get over the low wall into the rubbish on the other side.

Just before ten the team of horses, which had gone out earlier, returned noisily up the road, and although I did not look, I imagined they were towing some vehicle. When they had passed up toward the German stables, I stole a look out. I thought for a moment that the opportunity was ideal, for one of the searchlights was playing on the stableyard, probably to help the unhitching of the horses. I had just made the decision to go and was in the act of opening the door when some object clattered down the stairs behind me. A second later came the sharp order of the Corporal of the Guard as he turned his ten-o'clock relief up the road—I shivered as I realized how very nearly I had run right into them.

For fifteen minutes after the old guard had clattered past the door on their way to the guardroom, the searchlights on both ends were seldom still for more than a few seconds, but soon after that, the new sentries began to tire of their vigilance. Sitting back on the stairs, I could count up to four seconds while no light shone through the keyhole or under the door. So I opened the door cautiously and looked out.

Looking across the road, I realized that although the tower at the south end shone directly onto the exit, it would be the light from the roof of the hay shed that would be most dangerous, as it shone over the rubbish. I started counting the irregular breaks of darkness. Sometimes there would be one or the other searchlight shining on the road for over ten minutes, then for an erratic five minutes the road would be in darkness every few seconds.

"One—two—three," I counted, "one—two—three—four getting better now, one—two—three—four—my word, I could have made it that time, one—two—three—phew, just as well I didn't then . . ." And then there would be another period of light. The most unnerving thing about it all was the fact that there was no way of knowing how long any particular period of darkness was going to be. I knew that whenever I made the decision, it would be final. The success or failure of the whole plan depended on nothing more than luck.

I think perhaps I must have been poised there for half an hour. But it seemed years to me. I alternated between self-reproach for having missed a good chance and a chill of horror when a period of darkness lasted only one second.

And then I went. Not running, but carefully over the road, my stocking-covered shoes making little noise on the gravel. But as I perpared to throw myself over the low wall on the other side of the road, I sensed the return of one of the lights and involuntarily dropped to the ground, realizing instantly that I must present an ideal target to either sentry post.

First the light from the hay shed played idly up and down the road, and so brilliant was it that it shone right into the gravel where my face was buried. Then I sensed the other one flashing over my shoulder. My body tingled with terror, and for the first time in my life I felt the hairs on the nape of my neck pricking and rising.

I could hear two of the sentries talking quite clearly. They did not sound at all excited, and yet surely they must have seen me. My body began to flinch and cringe as I imagined a bullet striking home. My mind went numb, and I had no idea how long I lay there, but at last, one after the other, the lights swung away.

I sprang up. Instead of vaulting the low wall, I passed along it, turned into the courtyard of a military transport garage. I dropped behind a large oil drum as the first light swung back. Here I was not so frightened, for the low wall now shielded me completely from the one searchlight and the drum from the other. I must have been pinned there for all of ten minutes. It was uncomfortably cramped, and I was apprehensive lest some driver or late-returning guard should discover me.

But when darkness came, I was able to slip over the wall and worm through the rubbish toward the outer ring of wire. There was no need to stop even when both lights were playing down the road, for there was sufficient shadow among the rubbish and small scrub to mask cautious movement. There were thirty yards of this cover stretching over to the outer ring of double-apron barbed wire. This presented no problem with my wire cutters. But I was surprised when I was through it to run into a wire-netting fence. Following it along, I came to a break covered by a sheet of iron, which I crawled through to find myself in a small cleared space littered with large boxes. I was just passing one of the latter when a movement somewhere near stopped me. I hugged the ground, my heart in my mouth. All was quiet for a few minutes, then, just as I prepared to continue, again came the small movement, much closer this time. I placed it as just behind the box. I was becoming really scared when from inside the box came the unmistakable clucking of a disturbed hen. I was inside the guards' chicken run.

I crossed the run to the rear corner of the garage and cut a small square to let myself out. I found myself in a grass enclosure bounded by two very high stone walls, which ran into a corner some two hundred yards away. Very clearly I could hear the rumbling of the streetcars on the main Salonika road.

The wall bounding the road was about ten feet high, and I could see glass glistening along its length. But it didn't present any great obstacle—the Germans had attempted to make it more formidable by giving it an apron of barbed wire—thus making an ideal ladder.

I climbed up it carefully. The road was still very busy for that time of night. In addition to the streetcars and army vehicles, there was a steady stream of civilians and soldiers on both sides of the street. I waited ten minutes and was thinking of retiring for a few hours to let things settle down when I fancied I heard a single shot from back in camp. I listened for a full minute. Although I heard nothing further and was almost convinced that it was my overtaxed mind playing tricks, I decided to push on and take the chance of discovery.

With the glare from the lights of the prison camp, there was quite a shadow on the road side of the wall, and as soon as there was a perceptible break in the traffic below, I lowered myself as far as the lowest strand of barbed wire would allow me and dropped the remaining four feet, falling in a heap on the footpath.

My first reaction was one of acute pain. The jar was considerable. But almost immediately I became aware of two figures standing some fifteen paces away arguing volubly. They were both soldiers and I saw by the rifle he had slung over his shoulder that one of them was on duty. But as I picked myself up, I knew I had not been seen. The second soldier was obviously very drunk and was abusing the sentry roundly.

I moved quickly up the street for two or three hundred yards, stopped and removed the spare pair of socks that I had worn over my shoes, and walked very quietly into Salonika.

The whole of the venture up to this stage had been cool and methodical. A desperate fear of the risks had numbed my mind against any anticipation of success. But now at every step I felt welling within me a glorious exhilaration, an ecstasy so sweet that my eyes pricked with tears of gratitude. All the oppression, all the worry and boredom that had so weighed me down seemed to disappear as though they were taken like a heavy cloak off my shoulders. The air was pure and free.

For perhaps an hour I let my exuberance lead me drunkenly up and down strange streets. Every unsuspecting soldier I passed was a boost to my confidence. As each approached, I weighed up his size, darted a glance right and left for possible flight, and then, as we drew level, either made a great play of blowing my nose or whistled the one Greek tune I knew in what I hoped was a nonchalant manner. But soon I realized there was no need to regard each as a suspicious enemy—each was going about his own business, whether leave or duty; probably the last thought anyone had was that the stream of pedestrians might include an English officer.

Although there was some attempt at a blackout, the streets were full of gaiety. From every restaurant and wineshop came the laughter and music of the conquerors. Happy, and here and there inebriated, couples thronged the alleyways. At one street corner a lone violinist was playing old music rather sweetly. I felt wonderfully at ease, confident and vastly superior to all those in field-gray uniforms who had not the sense to recognize an enemy in their midst.

However, somewhere in the center of Salonika, the exhilaration quieted and allowed reason to prevail. I turned reluctantly to follow my plan of being well clear of the city by dawn. With some difficulty I oriented myself. Striking south, I moved through a suburb full of cheerful chatter and houses that glowed with homely light until I came to the foot of the great Salonika Hill. I followed up the same zigzag path trod by many a conqueror, sitting down occasionally on the stone steps to read and marvel at the beauty of the subdued lighting fringed by the sea below me. One by one the lights in the nearby houses went out as the city quieted down. By the time I reached the old Salonika wall with its massive gateways, all was quiet.

I sat down fifty yards from the gateway and watched for a while. All the exits to Salonika were under guard. Occasionally every civilian would be forced to produce his identity card, but this particular gate divided the city from one of its more modern suburbs. From somewhere in the prison camp had come the information that, with the large numbers passing to and fro, the sentries had become very slack.

The sentry on duty moved out of the shadow of the archway

and shifted his slung rifle from one shoulder to the other. A group of civilians, coming from a side street near the wall, passed through quietly, so I braced myself and slouched through after them, blowing my nose noisily; indeed, so interested was I in appearing nonchalant that I almost collided with a sentry who was moving across the archway. But he hardly glanced at me. And so I went through the last suburb and down to the outskirts of the town. I drew my coat close around me, for the wind was bitterly cold.

Soon there loomed ahead of me a massive gray building, and the path I was following took me quite close to it. Just as I passed from the moonlight into its shadow, without warning and so suddenly that it froze me to the spot, a harsh order rang out and there before me in the dark I could see the glint of a bayonet some five inches from my throat.

Slowly I raised my hands to my shoulders, and as my fear was replaced by an overwhelming disappointment, muttered miserably,

"English—*Engländer—Englezi.*"

What happened then was typical of any adventures in Greece, the "land of you-never-know." The rifle clattered to the ground, two hands reached up and grasped mine, and before my startled wits could register what was happening, a bristly face had planted a kiss on both my cheeks. In the dark I could see my new friend was in uniform. As I looked again at the silhouette of the imposing building, in whose shadow we stood, some memory of a conversation in the camp convinced me that I had run into a Greek policeman guarding the civilian jail. It was the first indication, and a surprise after my other experiences, to find that the Greek police were not necessarily pro-German.

But after the first emotional outburst had spent itself, fear seized him and immediately he fell to gesticulating violently and whispering urgent instructions. I gathered he wanted me to make myself scarce and also not to continue along the track I had been following. When I shrugged my shoulders in an expression of

The Land of You-Never-Know

hopelessness, he seized my arm and pointed to some lights in the far distance with repeated whispers of, "*Bon, kala, goot, bon, kala, goot.*"

Half an hour, over a bare and stony hillock, brought me to the lights, a group of perhaps thirty poor houses. Most of them were in darkness and quiet, but the lights I had followed indicated that someone was still afoot. I moved in to try my luck, and knocked at the door of the nearest house.

We say an Englishman's home is his castle; so it is with the Greek. He won't let the drawbridge down at night until he recognizes a friend. He peers furtively at you from the window on the left of the door, then from the one on the right, and finally decides through the keyhole and from your foreign jabber that you are no friend. And after that no amount of noise or knocking, no entreaties or threats will affect him. You will hear urgent whispers inside, and movement near the door, but you are lucky indeed if it opens.

I tried every house in the first group, whether lights shone or not, but always with the same result. I felt desolate and cold, and the unusual exercise was causing my wound to tug uncomfortably at my thigh. To make things more desperate, suddenly from one of the dark alleyways between two houses bounded a large village dog, fiercely growling and snarling. Three or four of its kind joined it, and I was forced to move warily along one of the walls with my boots ready and my heart in my mouth.

At first the brutes showed a certain caution, and would move back a yard or two if I made as though I had something to throw, but gradually, as their numbers swelled, they took confidence and started snapping at the cuffs of my trousers. The situation was ugly. There seemed no possibility of help from the dark, aloof houses, and I knew that to run would only bring them upon me in a ferocity far beyond my strength to combat. But in the end that is just what I did. Panic seized me and I ran full pelt down the rough street, with them all at my heels, until, seeing a flight of steps leading up to a small house, I ran frantically up and hammered on the door. The first of the dogs came halfway up the steps and paused, the remainder staying snarling and yapping below.

From inside some order was called, then repeated, then footsteps padded over and the door was flung open. The smallest of men, about five feet high, smiled up at me and spoke rapidly in Greek. With a gesture I said, "*Englezi*," and indicated the bristling dark forms below. With that unique fluttering of the hand that is the Greek beckoning, I was waved into a tiny living room.

In the center of the room, huddled around a tin of ashes on the top of which were a few live coals, were two more small people— an old lady and a young fellow. On my entry they both stood up and looked over inquiringly. The first one said something, which I took to be an introduction of sorts, and the old lady, dear fragile thing that she was, reached up and patted my arm. She sighed deeply, and suddenly I felt in that sigh all the sympathy I had been craving for so long. They indicated a chair, and as I collapsed into it, both body and mind relaxed into a relief that brought me almost to tears.

They fussed around me, talking excitedly to one another. A very stiff *ouzo* was followed by a meal they prepared from a cabbage out of their garden. They apologized in Greek, until even I understood that they had no bread in the house to give me. We all sat around the small tin of ashes, occasionally blowing on the four or five coals, and I tried to explain with my hands the adventures that led me to their door.

Finally they decided it was time for me to get some rest and ushered me into another equally small room. The smallness of the whole house was unbelievable. There were only two rooms, and neither was more than eight feet square. I was given the only bed in the house, and the brothers spread rugs on the floor beside me. As I stretched comfortably in the short bed, the old lady came around and patted my forehead, sighing deeply. She then murmured something over me, crossed herself reverently, and departed into the other room, where I could hear her preparing a bed on the couch. Even after the house became quiet, I could hear her deep sighs as I myself lay, sleep impossible, and tried to consider my position and convince myself that I had really succeeded. Occasionally a half-moon broke cloud and shone wanly through the tiny windows. Outside, the last of the dogs ceased its baying and left a peaceful stillness, made homely by the steady breathing of the two brothers on the floor. . . .

. . . This was by no means the end of Lieutenant Thomas's escape. On foot he found his way to Mount Athos, that strange and lovely peninsula in the Aegean Sea that for twelve hundred years has had no female, not even a female animal, among its population. Here he was hidden by the monks until with the help of another British escaper and a party of Greeks he stole a boat and set sail for Turkey. They were nearly shipwrecked on the voyage but finally reached Smyrna—and freedom.

Major W. B. Thomas, Distinguished Service Order, Military Cross and bar, United States Silver Star, is now a regular officer in the British Army.

8.

Jump for Freedom

Peter Medd, like David James, was rescued by his enemies from the sea. This time the enemies were Italian. As a pilot in the Fleet Air Arm, Lieutenant Medd was flying from the deck of HMS Warspite. In August, 1940, he was shot down into the Mediterranean.

His first prison camp was near Sulmona, the monastery camp from which Anthony Deane-Drummond made his first two escapes. Medd was moved from camp to camp in Italy until he found himself with George Millar at Gavi. This story begins when the Italians capitulated on September 8, 1943. . . .

. . . Armistice! We heard the news at eight o'clock on the evening of September 9. Down below, outside our small barred mess windows, there was an excited twittering from the Italian guards, cries of "*A casa!*" gestures of contempt for everything military. There were soberer feelings among the prisoners: feelings of relief that a long weary chapter had come to an end; feelings of expectancy, uncertainty, the realization that now we must think

Jump for Freedom

for ourselves again, and perhaps think quickly. There was no wild celebration—the *vino* had run out.

Our commandant, Giuseppe Moscatelli, known not the least bit affectionately to his charges as "Joe Grapes," had lived up to his reputation and left the camp in this important hour. We were in the hands of that incompetent pair of old dugouts, de Cesare and Odino, who refused to take any action until their colonel returned.

At seven o'clock next morning we were startled by a burst of tommy-gun fire and the boom of a grenade—Germans. Soon, a very demoralized Italian ration party returned to the camp bearing the corpse of one of their number. Jerry had done his job well, posting machine guns to cover the fortress before dawn, and now, truly appreciating the Italian character, striking terror and bringing demoralization by one quick act of brutality. The rest was easy. Joe Grapes handed over the entire camp, lock, stock, and barrel, to a German NCO and sixty men. Gavi Castle, true to its thousand-year-old tradition, had once more surrendered without a fight.

Followed four days of feverish thought and activity. We had been unable (except once) to find a way out; now one *must* be found in a hurry. A tunnel was started, to join a secret passage of which we had been told by a *carabiniere*. The diggers worked long hours desperately and promised us success. The tension was appalling: Would it be finished before they took us away?

The diggers forecast success for Monday night, September 13. Our hopes ran high; we began to think of "outside" instead of "how to get outside." Then came the bombshell. At ten o'clock on Monday morning it was announced that all officers would leave the camp in an hour's time. This possibility had, of course, been foreseen, and hiding places had been arranged for a certain number of us, in the hope that after we had left the Germans would evacuate the camp themselves. I had been allocated a bunk hole, but at the last moment it seemed to me that this was merely walking into a trap; there was no other exit, and the Germans, being in no hurry, would be quite prepared to wait and starve us out. But about fifty others hid up—too many, for Jerry was bound to notice the absence of that number.

And so the forlorn remnant left Gavi forever, more miserable even than when we had arrived at this gloomy fortress, stuggling down the hill with the fraction of our accumulated possessions that it was possible or permissible to take. Past the great sunflowers, whose heads seemed turned in shame, past the Italian officers' mess, where a little group of quislings gazed at us dispassionately, down the dusty winding road to a line of commandeered buses and trucks heading, strangely, toward France.

Now, for the first time, our captors realized that we were not all there, for the special seat reserved for the brigadier remained empty. A storm burst, which, for volume of noise and confusion, rivaled anything produced by Italians. It was four hours before the convoy left for Acqui, each truck guarded by three tommy-gunners and loaded with prisoners keyed to hair-trigger readiness to escape at the slightest opportunity, with a desperation which overcame all fear.

The greatest bogey to spontaneous escape is apathy. A fleeting opportunity occurs; you say to yourself: "No, a better opportunity is bound to occur soon." Or you suddenly think of the danger to the others, and, thinking, the chance slips by, never to return. You know you are determined to escape, but the starting friction is terribly hard to overcome. The secret of spontaneous escape is: Don't think—go.

On this long, uncomfortable truck ride, two successful breaks were made, simultaneously. The trucks were going slowly up a winding hill, with a wooded downslope on the left, when Frank Simms and Pitchford jumped. There was no shooting: the dusty tommy guns had jammed. For minutes there was no panic—the guards were bewildered. Then, of course, hell was let loose.

At Acqui we entrained, but there was a four-hour wait in the station before we left. During this time we were allowed to stroll on the platform. Tommy MacPherson made a daring dash for the road, and a shooting match started in the center of the town, ending with his recapture. Two months later I found Tommy had beaten me to England, having escaped from Germany into Sweden. No prisoner deserved success more, for his mind was passionately concentrated on thoughts of escape.

By now I was getting more desperate than ever, saying to myself that I *must* go, to justify my decision not to hide up, thinking back on three monotonous years, and forward to an unknown number of even more monotonous ones. But no opportunity seemed to come my way. Then, just before the train left, twelve of us were moved to a cattle truck near the back and locked in without guards. This truck had a sort of sentry box sticking up in the roof, with a window for the guard to look along the top. It seemed almost too good to be true.

We left Acqui at ten thirty in the evening. Now we had to move fast, for at Alessandria, in half an hour, we had to change trains. Quickly Captain Liebenberg and I broke the sentry box window, squeezed through and climbed down onto the buffers, he on the left side, I on the right. There we clung, waiting for the train to slow down, with a thrilling warm wind in our faces, and a wide, moonlit countryside rushing by, and an overflowing feeling of freedom and happiness in our hearts. Then, "Jump!" shouted Lieby, and I jumped.

I landed on hands and knees, and didn't even roll over—didn't even hurt myself. In a flash all my inhibitions about the risks of train jumping dissolved. We were passing through a cutting, and the bank on my side was too high to climb, so I lay alongside the rail, under the running board, and prayed that no inquisitive sentry would notice me as the last half of the train rumbled by. Then suddenly I found myself alone in the moonlight, with the train's red taillight quickly receding, and not a sign of Lieby. I climbed the other bank and set off rather aimlessly across the fields, my one idea being to get away from the railway. My sense of freedom was overlaid with a feeling of loneliness and bewilderment. Here was I, alone in the great open world for the first time in three years, dressed only in checked shirt, plus fours, stockings and shoes, my only possessions a tin of Ovaltine tablets and one hundred lire, for in the last-minute excitement my well prepared escape outfit was forgotten. Here was no comforting routine, no certainty, no solid foundation of prison-camp life to drug my senses. Now I must think, and act, and make decisions. The responsibility seemed overpowering.

So I walked to a farmhouse, told them how I had escaped, and asked for help. What a friendly welcome for a refugee! I was pressed into a chair, given bread and cheese and wine, surrounded by a crowd of inquisitive and excited people. Here was the *padrone* of the house and his family, and charming Mariuccia Pesca and her sister, evacuated from Genoa—the first girls I had been face to face with for three years—and one of their male admirers from a neighboring house.

We talked of escape, and Germans, and Mussolini, and my plans. They were pathetically optimistic: the British would land at Genoa in a few days, and my best plan was to get into "plainer" clothes and remain hidden in the district until rescued. I accepted, at least, the offer of plain clothes, and Mariuccia's boy friend took me to his house to get them.

There, his pretty young sister came down in her nightdress and found me more bread and cheese and wine, while I changed my too-English clothes for a worn black coat and trousers, a blue shirt, and Trilby hat. Then I left them—wished on my way by whispered *auguri* and bits of advice, touched and encouraged by such spontaneous generosity. Living in Italy as a refugee was not going to be so hard, after all.

I wandered up into the hills left of Acqui, reveling in the warm night, the full moon, the wide space and freedom. At last I made myself a bed in the bracken in a small coppice and fell asleep to the murmur of strange forgotten sounds—wind rustling through trees, an owl hooting, the distant bark of a watchdog. It was hard to distinguish where reality ended and dreams began. I half expected to see Titania appear.

The sun woke me, flickering through the leaves, casting long shadows across the bracken, stirring into life suspicious blackbirds and inquisitive lizards and industrious spiders who seemed intent on binding me to my brackeny couch.

I climbed to the top of the hill, where the wood ended, and vineyards began, with widely spaced farmhouses, still asleep. To the southeast, the slope dropped steeply to the Alessandria-Acqui Valley, containing the main road, railways, and river, with, beyond, a jumble of hills fading to the faint outline of the Gavi Mountains. To the south lay the main range of the Apennines, higher and more wild, stretching away to France. To the north the ground sloped down to the broad Po Valley, with, beyond, a suspicion of Alps, the great massif of Mont Blanc and Monte Rosa.

So I lay there till noon among the vines, feeding myself on fat red and white grapes, sweating slightly as the hot sun rose in a cloudless sky, watching the endless German convoys going south along the road, and trying to decide on a plan.

There were three choices. I might go to France. It was only fifty miles away, and the German guards had told us a landing had been made at Toulon. If not, one could probably get to Spain, but that would be a long way, and I couldn't be certain of help from the French. Or I might go to Switzerland. This was close, too—just eighty miles across the plain—but we had heard the Germans and Swiss were guarding the two sides of the frontier, and, anyway, once there, would one ever get out? Unlimited winter sports would be magnificent, but it wasn't war. Finally, there was the walk down through Italy to join our advancing army. With luck, they would do most of the walking. Little did I guess how wrong I was!

So I chose the third, but first I decided to go back to Gavi. The Germans might have evacuated it, and the boys hiding up might want the tip to come out. Then, David Stirling, one of the hidden, had selected a commando team, in which I was to practice guerrilla tactics in northern Italy. There might still be a chance of joining up and having our fun.

About noon I descended the hill, crossed the main road in a lull between convoys, and headed through the cornfields for the river, sheathed in its coat of tall poplars and thick undergrowth. There I found a ford, where the swift knee-deep water rushed in foam over the tumbled rocks, and waded across, feeling rather ridiculous under the placid stare of a couple of sleek white oxen.

Soon I reached a road again, and here I got my first fright. A sinister little man in a black hat—the swarthy aquiline type of Italian—said to me: *"Dove andate?"* ("Where are you going?") in that unpleasant tone of voice I had already learned to associate with fascists and *carabinieri*. I mumbled an unconvincing reply and hurried on as fast as I could with dignity, heading for the hills.

There, on the hillside, I found a white house, with a white-haired old man mending a wine cask outside the front door. I told him I was an escaped British prisoner and asked for help. He looked up fiercely. "How do you know I am not a fascist?" Then his blue eyes twinkled.

He was a retired merchant skipper, evacuated here from Genoa with his family. We went indoors and met his wife, thin and frail, and utterly worn out with years of too much work. This family—there was a daughter, too—was living on the starvation line. They had nothing, absolutely nothing. The neighboring farmers charged them fantastic prices for food, or refused to sell so they lived on the ration, which was inadequate and not always obtainable nowadays. Their Genoa home had been bombed, and here they lived in this empty house with a few salvaged bits of furniture and bedding. They suffered in silence. Her sympathy was all for me, a *poverino* who couldn't go home, and he never talked about hardships except to say gruffly that it was all their own fault for ever having put up with Mussolini. In this he was the most enlightened Italian I ever met.

The day faded. Mrs. Valente set about preparing supper, and

we went out onto the flat roof and looked at the landscape through a pair of ancient binoculars, the sort that every retired old sailor has, which shows two images and is unadjustable. There we talked of the sea dispassionately, for he showed no feelings of any sort. Yet I think he was glad to be able to talk once more with another sailor. Then we went into supper.

Polenta—the staple dish of the poor in northern Italy—tomatoes and walnuts. This is what they lived on. She apologized continually; he grunted and said nothing. After supper the daughter arrived, bringing a breath of fresh air into this rather embarrassing atmosphere. She worked in an office in Genoa: left home on foot at four thirty every morning on a two-hour walk to the station. (You daren't bicycle these days; the thing would be stolen within twenty-hour hours.) Then a two-and-a-half-hour ride in a cattle truck, owing to the shortage of rolling stock, would get her to the office about nine. There she worked until four thirty in the afternoon, when the long ride home began.

In spite of a sixteen-and-a-half-hour day, she had a freshness and gaiety about her that were charming. As she described her day, there was never a hint of hardship or overwork. Her Italian accent would have penetrated an air-raid shelter; her Genoese dialect was quite incomprehensible. She had brought back the week's ration of flour, sugar, and salt. Each pathetic little package was unwrapped with the excitement of a child over a Christmas stocking. We all went to bed early, for the next morning we had to get up at four. I had a mattress on the floor of the old man's bedroom and slept like a log.

The alarm clock woke us punctually, and we breakfasted off hot milk and stale bread in the pungent light of an acetylene lamp. Mrs. Valente, her daughter, and I left the house at four thirty for the long walk to the station. I don't know whether the chaperoning was on account of me: the old women excused herself by saying she made the trip every day.

My way lay eastward toward Ovada, so I left them short of the station and set off along the road in the pale dawn light. For the first half hour I met nobody, but then the countryside began to wake up. Sleepy bullock carts rumbled by, the fields seemed imperceptibly to sprout with peasants engaged in the eternal task of hoeing. I was glad to find I raised no curiosity in them. But as the morning activity increased I decided to leave the road—it was the sight of a German ambulance parked by the curb just ahead that finally decided me—and traveled eastward across a country of steep hills and gullies, vineyards on the slopes, and thick undergrowth in the hollows. My lunch was a handful of walnuts and some stolen grapes, eaten in the sunshine in the dry bed of a stream.

About noon I reached Ovada. Here, I remembered, was a German headquarters; the place had been stiff with troops when we came through three days before. I sneaked across the main road and under the railway by a culvert, and so up into the wooded hills to the south. This was not the most direct way to Gavi, but I wanted to reach the main west-east ridge of the mountains, where going would be easier and safer than among the foothills, with their crisscross systems of rivers, roads, and railways.

By now the sun had vanished in a white haze, which darkened and condensed to torrential rain. Even this did not lessen my unaccustomed joy of freedom. There were more pleasures to be rediscovered among these woods: the intoxicating scent of damp pine needles, the sight of bright-eyed little birds hopping silently through the undergrowth, the sudden explosion of disturbed partridges taking to the air, or of a startled hare zigzagging across the hillside. These were strange, exciting sensations for me, and I thought to myself, in the old familiar words, "Ain't nature wonderful?" It was not until days later that I realized the absolute paucity of wildlife in Italy. A similar countryside of woods and mountains in England would teem with life, yet here in Italy one sometimes walked a whole day without seeing flesh or fowl, save the vulgar crow wheeling overhead, and lizards and snakes scuttling for cover. I never saw a rabbit in Italy, except a tame one. There were a few hares and partridges, fewer squirrels and pheasants. Even the small birdlife is practically nonexistent, for every Italian countryman carries a shotgun, and anything over the size of a sparrow is fair game to him. There are laws, indeed —shooting begins officially on October 1—but all laws, the Italian believes, are made to be broken. This year the German requisitioning of all firearms will probably give Italian wildlife such a chance as it has never had before, though even this order, carrying the death sentence as penalty for disobedience, is only being partly carried out.

Up there, in the mist and woods, I lost my sense of direction, so I decided to go down and take shelter in a farmhouse. I found one in a fold of the hill, almost overgrown by the wood, attached to a tiny vegetable garden and vineyard, which seemed the only means of support for the swarm of dirty children and old women who filled the single ground-floor room. They gave me bread and wine, and gazed at me in wonder, tremendously intrigued to meet an Englishman for the first time. Then, the rain having stopped, a small child guided me down to the river and across the Ovada–Genoa railway, and left me to climb into the oak woods on the other side, northeastward toward Gavi.

A quarter of an hour later, as I was passing a farmhouse, an old man came out and called, "Come in, *giovanotto*, and have a drink." I refused, for it was getting late and I had far to go, but he insisted. His son, he said, had just reached home from France, where he and his fellow soldiers had been ordered to lay down their arms after the armistice. When I admitted I was English, the soldier turned to me and said earnestly, "Never tell that to anyone. The country is full of fascist spies. Say you are a soldier of the Italian Fourth Army, disbanded in Toulon, returning to your home in Trieste. Your accent will pass for a Triestino in this part of the country."

This was interesting. I hadn't realized till then that Italy is such a honeycomb of self-contained cells, each having its own customs and speaking its own dialect, that country people are easily fooled by the accent of a "foreigner" from a different part of the country.

Shortly afterward, on the road to Gavi, I had an opportunity of trying this out. An old peasant attached himself to me, and we walked together for five miles, discussing every sort of subject, and to the end he believed me a good Triestino who had laid down his arms in the service of his country, and was now going to the only sensible place for an Italian—home.

This road led us along the crest of a tortuous range of hills, scarred by deeply eroded gullies and cut by streams. Here and there in this desolate landscape were fantastic villages, perched on the very tops of rocky pinnacles, secure from the invader of olden days who ravaged their vineyards and fields on the lower slopes.

The rain had cleared and left a fine, steamy-blue evening. The old familiar Gavi landmarks drew slowly closer. The peasants were going home, many of them heading for their nearest village, taking their firearms to be handed in to the German command, or local *podestá* (mayor). One man passed us, almost hysterical with anger, waving a big .45 revolver, and crying that he had tried to hide it, but had been denounced.

At last Gavi Monastery came in sight, winking like a lighthouse in the setting sun. I climbed its winding ramp in the dusk, considerably excited at seeking refuge so near to the lion's den.

After the armistice, our Italian chaplain had told us that, in the event of escape, we could safely ask for help at any monastery, and that he would warn Gavi Monastery to expect refugees. I didn't know whom to ask for or where to go, and before I knew where I was, found myself face to face with a white-coifed nun. I asked for the priests' quarters and foolishly told her that I was an escaped British prisoner—so soon had I forgotten the soldier's advice. In a moment the news had reached all the women, and even the children in the attached orphanage heard about it and came to peer at me around corners.

Then I met the father. He led me to the ramparts and looked at me a long time without saying a word. Then he asked, "Are you a Catholic?" "No, a Protestant," I confessed, and felt for a moment that I was going to be turned shamefully away, an infidel and outcast. "Never mind," he said, "we offer shelter to everybody." We stood in silence gazing across the valley to where Gavi Castle reared its gloomy shadow out of the mist, the very embodiment of all that is evil and sinister. The arc-lights glinted balefully: so the Germans were still in occupation. I thought miserably of those unfortunate fellows who lay hidden there, walled up in cold, dank holes, unable to talk or light a match, or move about, wondering whether Jerry was still there or not, wondering whether the next moment would bring a hand grenade bouncing down on them. And I was very glad of my decision not to hide up.

The father was talking in a low, precise voice. It was a reprimand to me for spreading the news that I was English. "Those women cannot hold their tongues. Already the news may be down in the village. The Church is always suspect, and we are closely watched here."

I was beginning to be quite windy. But that was nothing to what was to come. I was told to hide in the garden while he removed the watchdog from the side door. Then we crept quickly in on tiptoe, up the stairs to his room, and locked ourselves in. Soon there was a knock at the door. "Who is it?" asked the priest, and there was a mumbled reply from outside. "Well, you can't come in now, I am busy," said the priest in a tone of voice that would have raised curiosity and excitement in the dullest listener. If there were any who hadn't heard of my arrival from the nun, they would soon learn now that there were strange goings-on in Gavi Monastery that night.

When the steps had died away, he led me on an inspection of the bolt holes. "You see," he said, "we have two exits from this place. If they come by this door, you creep down the stairs, through the vestry, and out the back. If they come by the back door, I'll keep them talking until you can get out the side door. And just to be quite certain, we'll hang this rope out of the pantry window, and you can climb down that."

By this time I was thoroughly jittery, seeing a German around every corner. Then suddenly I realized that this good man was enjoying himself as never before. The traditional monastic spirit of intrigue flowed in his veins. This promised to be the best thing that had happened in Gavi since the days of the Borgia Pope. I laughed to myself and went up to enjoy my supper with a quiet heart.

I ate alone—steaming *minestra*, bread, cheese, and wine—watched by the father and another priest. They told me the Germans showed no signs of leaving the castle, but so far had caught no prisoners. We talked little, for I was very tired.

The father's quarters consisted of a sitting room, bedroom, and pantry. The inside wall of the sitting room had a window giving out into the chapel. In this room they made me up a bed on a couch; spring mattress and clean sheets, and two pillows. As I slipped into this heaven of softness, a boy started to play the organ, slow quiet chords. The dangers of life seemed infinitely remote. I went to sleep with the peace of mind of the medieval refugee who sought sanctuary at the altar and knew he was safe. Even the rope in the pantry window couldn't keep me awake.

The good father woke me at four thirty, and I think he was disappointed the night had been so uneventful. While I ate my bread-and-wine breakfast, he gave me his advice. He suggested I go and call on the parish priest of a nearby village, Alice. "He is a well-informed man, who knows the country and always listens to the English broadcasts."

I slipped down the hill in the half-light, before the inquisitive nuns were awake, and took the road eastward to Alice. Away over on the left was the somber fortress of Gavi, brooding over its secrets. Neither hill nor wood seemed to hide me from the baleful stare of those arc-lights.

The sun was up when I reached Alice, and Mass was about to begin as I entered the vestry and introduced myself to the *parroco* (vicar). He was fat and genial, his face full of an owlish wisdom, and his eyes twinkled as he heard my story. He thought for a while, suggested a course of action at great length, canceled it, and thought again. From time to time a black-veiled woman would come in and urge him to begin the Mass, but his mind was on more worldly matters now. Then he began talking again. It was his opinion, too, that I should stay around here and wait for a nearby landing, and he suggested the name of a family, who lived way up in the hills, who would look after me or pass me on to their relations. I decided to go there; perhaps it would be possible to get passed on from house to house, right down to the British lines. I had no faith at all in the theory of a British landing up this end of the country.

So I left him to say his Mass, and was pulled into the kitchen by his niece (the rectory, in country Italy, is attached to the church) and served with hot milk and bread. She was also an evacuee from Genoa. Her enthusiasm for Britain, and her desire to help me, were most reassuring. I began to realize that I was in a friendly country.

On I went, then, across the tiny stream in its wide bed of smooth white pebbles, where the village women were already ranged on their knees, pounding their dirty linen, and up the other bank through the vineyards to pleasant oak woods. Here was a *riserva di caccia*—a game reserve—which seemed to contain more game than the unrestricted areas, in spite of occasional shots in the distance.

At last I found my house—the Casa Brucciata—a neat, clean farmhouse sitting on a green, undulating grassy alp. There was suddenly something rather Swiss about the scene, a change from the nearby oak woods.

In the doorway sat an old woman peeling potatoes. I told her of my visit to the parson and introduced myself as an escaped British prisoner. "How can you prove it?" she said suspiciously. This was a bit difficult, because I had no identity marks. The letter addressed to me at Gavi which I had saved for this very purpose was still in my coat on the way to Germany.

"Well, I can't prove it, but I certainly am English." My ingenuousness must have convinced her, for she softened a bit. Then I asked her if I could stay, as the priest had said, and she was again cautious in her reply. "You must wait until the men return. You understand, I, too, am under orders here."

So I went out onto the grassy mountainside and slept in the sun until lunchtime. I got back to the house just as the men were coming in from work. I and my story were received gravely, but with great politeness. I could see they weren't particularly taken with the idea of putting me up, or passing me on to friends, and I wondered what my next move should be.

Lunch was now ready, and we went into the kitchen. The *padrone*—the old woman's husband—took the end of the table, and motioned me to a place on his right. At the other end of the table sat his two sons and a youth of about fourteen. An immense bowl of steaming *minestra* was placed before the father, and he filled my plate and his. Then the other men helped themselves. It is delicious, filling stuff, this *minestra*, made of macaroni, potatoes, beans, herbs, sometimes bits of meat, all mixed into the consistency of Irish stew. We had three helpings each. (Second and third helpings are the rule in Italy; what a pity it is considered greedy at home!) We drank water, the *padrone* and I having a glass each, the remainder drinking from a huge ladle, which they dipped into a central bowl. When all the men had finished eating, the *minestra* was removed and the women got down to their share —not much, for there wasn't much left—which they ate sitting on stools in corners, or standing. Then all the men got up and went upstairs for two hours' *siesta*, with never a word to me.

This was my first introduction to Italian peasant society. The feudal primitiveness of it is almost terrifying. Man is a god, the head of the family a supergod. The women are servants, never speaking in the presence of men unless spoken to, never pushing themselves forward, working ceaselessly from before dawn to dusk, uncomplainingly. They know their position; it would never enter their heads to try to alter it.

The woman had told me that many Italian soldiers passed the Casa Brucciata on their way home, so I decided to await the afternoon in the sun and attach myself to any party who would have me. Living in this austere family would be impossible, I realized, and, anyway, it wouldn't help me to join with our army.

About three o'clock a party of five arrived at the farm, singing and chattering like a covey of magpies. They welcomed me enthusiastically. They were going to Rome, and of course I could come along with them.

We swapped stories in front of the farmhouse, while they munched the bread given them by the old woman. Then suddenly, with no apparent word of command, they were off again up the path to Rome, laughing and shouting, and I with them.

Carlo, Giuliano, Augusto, Giuseppe, and Renzo. It was Renzo Baccani who invited me to come along. He attached himself to me almost as personal bodyguard, taught me the peculiar ways of Italian soldiers, steered me through many dangers, and shared everything he possessed with me. Carlo Bergamino was our leader. He might have been the original Charlie Chaplin: the little cane, the outsize trousers, the absurd moustache. He walked in decrepit sandals. And on top of this music-hall personality he had a superb power of command, which enabled him more or less to control his irresponsible companions and to stifle at source the many embryo arguments.

We had only walked for ten minutes from the Casa Brucciata when the whole team suddenly stopped, unpacked their lunch, and settled down to a huge lunch of bread and cheese and tinned fish, in which I was compelled to join. But ten minutes later Carlo had us on the road again.

We climbed to the top of our particular mountain, from which we looked down into a deep valley, and beyond the imposing massif of the big mountain that dominates the Gavi landscape. Down to the right, the valley led away to Voltaggio, and this was our direction.

Voltaggio presented a certain danger. We knew it to be full of

Germans, yet there was no avoiding the town. But here again we were lucky. A charming Genoa evacuee attached herself to us and offered to guide us through the town by safe back streets.

On the far outskirts of the town we stopped again and said good-bye to our fair guide. An admiring crowd of spectators collected around us, and the whole story of the escape from France had to be retold.

These soldiers belonged to the Italian Fourth Army, garrisoning Toulon. On the signing of the armistice, the general had ordered his men to lay down their arms and confined them to barracks. There followed a mass breakout by the troops, who stormed the doors with hand grenades. The fugitives took the train to Turin (still in Italian hands), where they broke up into small parties, changed into plain clothes, and started the long trek to their homes.

We were about to move on to find a lodging place for the night farther from the town when the *padrone* of the nearby farmhouse invited us to stay with him. We accepted. It was convenient, for here close to the farm flowed the river, and we were able to have a bath and wash our clothes. Then we sat on the stoop in the twilight talking to our hosts, and two lovely evacuees brought us *vino*. They drew me aside and said, "You are not Italian, are you? American or English?" Then one of them told me she was engaged to an Italian naval officer, Lieutenant Casinaghi, and would I please call on him when we crossed the line, for he had gone to Malta with the Italian fleet, and she had had no news of him for a long time. I realized then it was no good trying to fool an educated Italian with my accent.

I fell in love with these girls from Zena; in fact all the Genoese girls I had met. Their soft accent is delicious. They know how to make themselves attractive in a not-too-sophisticated way, in spite of the rigors of war. There is a practical good sense about them, so different from the hothouse-plant type that one associates more with this Mediterranean climate. They reminded me of the

English girls of Shanghai: vivacious, hard-working, with an immense appreciation for life.

Then we had supper—a hugely amusing supper. The *vino* flowed, the *minestra* came again and again in steaming platefuls, and Carlo and Augusto kept up a cross-talk—mostly in different dialects—which kept the company in fits of laughter. Augusto has one passion: catching chickens. He dreams and talks all day about catching chickens. And now he described, in brilliant fashion, his failures and successes in this line since leaving Turin.

Finally, we were shown to bed in the loft, all rather tipsy and hysterical. Life seemed good. We were free, we were going home. Soon—any day now—the British would land at Genoa, and there would be no more war, but instead unlimited food and luxuries and work for all. Poor, self-deceiving Italy! . . .

. . . Peter Medd walked with his "crazy gang" for several days until, in a small village, they met Maj. Frank Simms of the Royal Warwickshire Regiment, who had escaped earlier on the journey from Gavi. Together the two Englishmen walked seven hundred miles in forty days to meet the advancing Allies. It was indeed a "long walk home."

Lieutenant Commander Peter Medd, M.B.E., Royal Navy, was killed in a flying accident in August, 1944, before he had finished writing his book. The narrative was completed by his fellow escaper, Major Simms.

9.

Through Enemy Lines

Winton K. Sexton dedicated his book to the courageous men and women of Italy who helped him in his escape. It is the tribute of a brave man to equally brave men and women of the other side. The people of Italy had a fascist government which many of them hated, and war for the Italians was not the same thing that it was for us or for our Allies. It is difficult for us, who have never lived under a government imposed by force, to appreciate the feelings of men and women who would hide and aid an escaping enemy airman. The penalty of capture for Lieutenant Sexton, USAF, was return to the prison life from which he had escaped: for the Italians who had helped him it was death.

Lieutenant Sexton was a pilot in an American bomber squadron and was on his thirtieth mission when he was shot down on a bombing raid over Sicily. Badly wounded, he was picked up by the Germans and sent to a hospital in Italy. When the Allies landed and Italy capitulated, all the prisoners who were patients in the hospital were removed by rail to Germany.

Although he had a broken leg encased in plaster and several other unhealed wounds, Winton Sexton jumped from his train before it reached the Brenner Pass, seven hundred miles behind *the enemy lines. During the next nine months he made his way slowly down the length of Italy toward the advancing Allied armies. This account opens when he is within a few miles of his own troops camped on the outskirts of Anzio....*

... The next morning I got my hands on a pair of field glasses. For the next two days I sat on a high rock, planning an approach to the lines. I would gaze over the area until I saw some activity and would put a dot on the map at that location. In two days I had a line of dots, and by drawing a line through them I had a fair battle line to work with.

With the help of my battle line I planned an approach. The Germans had flooded several thousand acres of land about five miles south of the lines, and because of this there was little fighting there—more of a hold action. I decided to work south between the water and the lines and find a hole to get through. If I would go in a straight line to the front, I could walk the distance, if uninterrupted, within two hours, but to buck the line there would put me directly into Cisterna, the point of heaviest fighting.

The Italian with whom I was staying walked up one afternoon and asked what I planned to do. He looked for a while at the front, and then pointed to a pond out on the plain about a mile out on my course. "See that pond," he said. I noticed. "You'll be caught before reaching it." I was through arguing with all these people, so I said nothing. Since escaping from the Germans, I had walked over five hundred miles through "hell and high water," and I wasn't going to sit down now, just ten miles from freedom.

My plans for an approach to the lines were just as thorough as possible. I had to walk about ten miles in order to work into the position I had planned to crack the line. Considering the distance and the very slow speed I would make, I allowed myself four days to get this position. As provisions, I took one loaf of bread, two large links of sausage, a couple of ounces of sugar, and a pint of alcohol distilled from wine. None of this was to be eaten unless

I got pinned down and couldn't move. I knew there were a few Italians still living in the battle area, and they were to supply me with food whenever possible.

On the afternoon of March 25, 1944, I decided I was ready. That night I checked and oiled my automatic, wrote a note to be given to the American troops in case I wasn't successful, and went to bed.

At four the following morning, I set off down the mountain. The front was relatively quiet, with sporadic firing.

By daybreak I was down on the plain. It was unusual not to see a flock of Italians going into the fields at dawn. Most of the population had evacuated the area, leaving behind their empty homes and unplanted fields.

About midday I spotted an Italian family milling around a *capanna*—a cabin along the path ahead. They were friendly, and I had my first meal out on the Pontine flats that Mussolini had converted from swampland into a fertile asset to the country. According to these people there were Germans billeted in many of the vacant houses over the area. They were in the front lines one day and back resting the next. Evidently they were not being pushed too hard in this section of the front, which was my reason for picking the south line to cross.

Later in the afternoon I passed a house with three "Jerries" sunning themselves in the yard; but they paid no attention to the peasant as he nonchalantly trudged down the path. They probably remarked how foolish anyone was to stay around risking death if he didn't have to. The peasant agreed with them!

By dusk the first night I had made remarkable progress. Long before noon I had even passed the pond I wasn't to reach at all, and also succeeded in finding another family with whom I stayed for the night.

With the break of dawn, I was off on my second day. I soon came to the Via Appia—this new road to Rome. To the north, the Allies had cut this highway and were holding about a mile of it. I had to walk about a half mile south along it to cross a canal on the west side. This section of road had been under fire, for it

Through Enemy Lines

was covered with splintered trees and shell holes. I didn't consider it wise to stay around there any longer than necessary. It a way it was nice to be so close to our troops but, on the other hand, it wasn't particularly safe.

By midafternoon I was lying on a clump of grass a few feet from the Mediterranean. I had hit the coast about three miles south of the town of Sabaudia, which I decided was just about on the line. I stayed for a while just looking out into the sea. I closed my eyes and listened to the waves lap the shore. I could hardly realize that men were dying just three miles north of this peaceful spot. Why couldn't I find a small boat and after dark row three miles up into friendly waters! The wind was coming out of the west, and that, along with the waves, would be a terrific fight. No, it was too risky, at least for now. Finally, I backtracked about one-fourth mile and then started slowly north toward the line. I spent the night in an evacuated house. It was equipped with blackout shutters, so after dark I made a fire and was quite comfortable. That night for the first time I was able to hear sporadic small-arms fire. The artillery was not firing south but was fairly heavy all night. I estimated that I was within two miles of the line.

Then next morning I moved about a half mile north and met an Italian. I was able to get some milk and a little bread from him. He advised me to get out of the area because the Germans had organized a battalion of Italian fascists and were moving in to defend that sector. They were taking billets in all the vacant houses and were questioning everyone they met. About noon I found a two-story house that was still vacant, so I went upstairs and spent the afternoon looking over the country around me.

Sabaudia was about a mile to the northwest, and I could see the town of Littoria about four miles to the east. I saw little activity in the area. It was evident that if there were Germans around, they were all right in the front line. Just after dusk I walked another half mile north and snooped around until I found another vacant house. I was awakened several times during the night by trucks passing the house, but none stopped. Just before dawn an artillery duel started, and I moved to a room downstairs. Being unable to sleep for the noise, I walked outside to watch the show. To my amazement, I noticed that the German artillery was firing from quite a distance behind me, and the shells were arching overhead.

The German shells were landing about a mile north of me, so I judged the front lines to be between a half mile and a mile away.

As dawn came I went back into the house, sat by an upstairs window, and looked the situation over. The town of Sabaudia was just a half mile west of me and was separated from the sea by a long lake. About noon I could hear mortar fire and noticed that the Germans were firing at a point on the sandbar separating the sea from Sabaudia. Immediately, our troops put up a smoke screen that blanketed the area for the entire afternoon.

At dusk I set out for Lake Sabaudia, our troops being on the other side. It took me about three hours to walk the half mile to the lake shore. Every foot was dangerous, for it was necessary to pass through the German mortar line, and I wasn't sure where it was located.

Just as I reached the water's edge, the Germans fired a flare over the lake. I covered my face and lay motionless until the flare was extinguished. The Germans were afraid our troops were sending patrols across in rubber boats, for about every fifteen minutes a flare went up. Somewhere along the shore there were Jerry guards, and as far as I knew I might have been lying right next to one.

It was pitch black, and the call of an occasional night bird was the only sound audible. I lay for a time, not knowing what to do. By swimming fast, I could cross the lake in five minutes; but the noise would bring another flare, followed by a stream of bullets—just like shooting fish in a barrel. It was March, and the water was still ice cold to the touch, making slow swimming hazardous.

I decided after a time to try swimming dog fashion across the lake. I took off my clothes and hid them, together with my automatic, under a bush. I then got the bottle of alcohol out of my knapsack and consumed the contents, hoping that the alcohol would help to limit the effects of the cold water.

The Germans fired another flare out over the water, and in a few seconds, everything was black. I quietly let myself into the water and soon became so numb that I could hardly move. I started swimming out slowly, with just my head above the water. After only about a hundred feet the startling realization that I would never reach the opposite shore struck like a bolt of lightning! Because of making noise, I couldn't swim fast enough to keep my circulation up and I was beginning to cramp. I turned and, using every ounce of energy at my command, was barely able to make it back to shore. I groped around in the darkness until I had found my clothes and automatic. After dressing I fell on the ground, completely exhausted. I was stuck and I knew it! It would be suicide to attempt to crack the line there by land. The Germans, as well as my own troops, were well dug in, and the area between them was heavily mined. If there were a battle in progress, with some movement in the line, it would be somewhat easier to cross, but Anzio was quiet.

Suddenly I heard voices, and before I could move, a Jerry patrol passed within a few feet of me. I didn't know if the Germans were looking for me or not, and didn't care much about it then. As soon as they were out of hearing distance, I crawled inland a few hundred feet, and then walked back to the house I had stayed in last.

There was a canal running by the house, and a bridge crossed within a few feet of it. About noon the next day, our artillery started firing on this bridge. The first shell landed about one hundred feet short of the bridge, and for the next ten minutes I was busy getting away from the house. They finally succeeded in hitting the house, but they failed to damage the bridge.

That same afternoon I did some serious thinking. The way things stood, it was just a matter of time before I would get caught playing around the front lines. If the Jerries didn't catch me, I'd probably get hit by Allied fire.

I got my map out and studied the situation. I knew the Allies would try to break out of the Anzio beachhead. The question was: Where would they head for then? However, it wasn't hard to see that Rome was the greatest prize left in Italy.

According to my map, I was about forty miles due south of Rome, but to get there I had to go back east at least ten miles in order to circle the main spearhead of the beachhead.

I wasn't too sure that I could get into Rome, but I decided to try. I certainly wasn't getting anywhere down here.

Two days later I was still sixteen miles from Rome. I was tired and hot, and my feet were a mass of blisters. I would walk a few hundred yards and then sit down, unable to go farther.

One of the times I was resting with my shoes off, a German soldier not over seventeen years old came walking over a hill with a gas can in his hand. Any attempt to put my shoes on and rush off would be obvious, so I just sat there studying him as he came up. I did manage to slip my automatic between the folds of a jacket I had in my lap.

"*Signor,*" he said and then asked a question in German. It was obvious he had run out of gas somewhere up the road and was asking me in German where a gasoline dump was along the road.

"*Signor,*" I said in my best and fastest Italian, "I have come a long way and am not familiar with these parts. You might inquire at that house," I said, pointing down the road. He didn't seem to understand what I was saying, but did catch on about the house.

"*Grazie,*" he said with a smile and walked on down the road.

I just sat there, rubbing my burning feet and watching him swing his gas can. "What the hell," I thought to myself, "I don't give a damn anymore."

Finally, I came to one of the main highways leading into Rome. The dome of St. Peter's was visible now to the west, but feeling as I did, I could never make it. I sat down on the shoulder of the highway and watched the steady stream of Italians coming and going, with an occasional German truck making a dash for it between Allied air patrols.

As I was sitting there, an elderly man and a boy on a bicycle stopped to rest. They immediately started a conversation, which

Through Enemy Lines 179

I took up, but of course they knew I was not an Italian. I told them I was going to Rome and asked how to get by a German road block that I knew was somewhere ahead. They told me where it was but also stated that the Jerries checked the identification cards of everyone passing in and out of Rome. There was no chance of going around the block, at least not until dark.

The boy asked if I had an identification card, and I answered, "Yes." However, I didn't exactly want to show it to the Germans. When I showed it to the boy and the old man, they understood.

The boy told me that just over the hill was a streetcar line that ran into Rome. He said the Germans weren't in the habit of checking it and suggested I take it into Rome. I laughed at this idea, but the more I thought about it, the better it sounded. I was feeling bad anyhow, and it had been a long time since I had been on a streetcar. Besides that, the old man was going to ride the bicycle into Rome and the boy would accompany me. What a nice deal this was going to be!

When we arrived at the station, there was a handful of people waiting. I instructed the boy that when the streetcar came he was to buy my ticket and then pay no attention to me, just in case something happened.

While we were sitting there, a British Spitfire patrol flew over. I asked the boy if they ever strafed the streetcar, and he said that the car always stopped under a tree when they were flying over.

Finally we saw the car coming, and everyone started out to the track. I followed the boy into the car, he paid two fares, and we sat down together.

It was a wonderful feeling to see the miles click by and not have to walk every one of them!

Just as we came into the outskirts of Rome, the streetcar started slowing down. Before I could figure out what was happening, it had stopped and a German guard was at each landing. There was nothing to do but sweat it out. Two Jerries came through the car, but instead of asking for identification cards, they were checking bundles that people were carrying! I had nothing but a light jacket; and although they checked the bundle of food my friend was carrying, they just looked at me and went on to the next seat.

After they had left I looked at my pale friend and let out a whistle. As soon as the streetcar started up again the boy asked the conductor what the idea was. He told him that they only checked bundles on every other trip—the other times, they checked identifications! I almost passed out when I heard that.

The streetcar took us right downtown. Rome is a beautiful city with a surprising number of ultramodern shops and cafés.

War hadn't come to the heart of Rome as yet, and the people, as they hurried here and there, seemed strikingly similar to those of New York, Chicago, or Kansas City. I began to feel as if I were home, and I wanted to drop a nickel in the nearest phone and ask the operator to give me Harrisonville, Missouri, and quick. Then I was going to shave, take a bath, and find the biggest steak a cow ever wiggled at a farmer. Well, at least it didn't hurt to think about those things.

Finally we came to the end of the line, and the boy said we would transfer to another car that would take us to his home.

We passed by the famous Colosseum and over the river. The boy's parents were evidently well-to-do, for they lived in a very nice brick apartment house.

While waiting for the father to arrive on his bicycle, I bathed my feet and went to sleep. About 7 P.M. he arrived, and we had dinner. I couldn't eat much because of a headache and fever. After dinner I asked the father about several addresses in Rome that I had acquired. He had at one time been an employee of the city, so he knew about where each address was located. However, he thought I should try to get into Vatican City rather than take a chance on the leads that I had given him. I laughed when he mentioned the Vatican as a place to go. It was common knowledge that there were a number of American boys there, but they had all "crashed" the gate and were just lucky. Anyway, I was so sick and my feet hurt so badly that I could have hardly walked in—much less run in!

Instead of discouraging me, he kept telling me ways he thought

I could get into the "free city." The more he talked, the better the deal sounded. There was one dangerous drawback in any plan, however. The German Secret Service in plain clothes were constantly milling around the place, and any suspicious actions by anyone were immediately checked. With this in mind, any plan to get into the Vatican could be dangerous. Once put into operation, the plan had to "click," for if there was any slipup it would all be over very quickly.

I asked in detail about the famous Swiss guards that were constantly on duty at all the entrances and came to the conclusion that they were there to protect the Vatican. I had no intention of harming the Vatican—all I wanted was to gain entrance, and I wondered what their reaction to that would be.

For years the people with whom I was staying had attended Mass at St. Peter's. They were familiar with what went on at the main entrance to the left of their famous cathedral. Also, it was possible to telephone into the Vatican from any place in Rome; but, of course, the SS probably were listening.

I knew that our government, as well as England and Germany, had an ambassador in the Vatican; and I began to wonder just how much fruit a few minutes of conversation with our ambassador would bear. Calling in from an outside station would be too dangerous, so this idea was shelved for the time being.

At 9 A.M. the following day, the boy and I were sitting at a table in a coffee shop across the street from an entrance to the Vatican—just about two hundred yards to the right of the main entrance. I was still sick with a terrific headache and fever and feared I had contracted malaria in the swamps near Anzio. I gave myself a full day before I would be flat on my back. I was desperate!

The boy's father knew an operator that worked on the Vatican radio station. He called him and asked him to come to the gate across from the coffee shop where we were. I wrote a note to be given to the American ambassador inside and gave it to the old man.

In a few minutes the operator appeared at the gate and my

friend went to meet him, and in a few minutes was back, saying that the note would be delivered, and for us to wait.

The boy recognized two SS men who came in and sat down for a cup of coffee. We paid our check and leisurely walked out of the place, going south toward the columns that form a circle around St. Peter's.

"I know both of the guards there at the main gate," the boy said. "Why don't I go see what they can do for you?"

"What if they tell the SS?" I asked.

"They wouldn't do that," he said. "I'll go up and talk to them, and if everything goes all right, I'll motion for you to come up."

"Good luck," I whispered as he started off.

I watched him as he went toward the huge fountain and on up the driveway to the left of St. Peter's.

I noted the friendly greeting exchanged between the guards and my friend, and I knew he was getting down to business. After a time they walked to a door to the right of the main entrance and, as they went in, the boy motioned to me to come up.

I was shaking like a leaf now. I didn't know if I was walking into a trap or not. I sat there for a minute, afraid to go, but I had to, there was no question about it.

I stood up and started off toward the entrance. I suppose it was a quarter of a mile across the huge square and I fully expected to be nailed by the SS before reaching the gate. I made my approach just as casual as possible, looking at the columns, the fountain, and acting the role of a tourist as much as possible. To me it seemed that the eyes of Rome were upon me, but that was a natural feeling.

I approached the small entrance and boldly walked in. Inside I found my friend talking to the guard, in fact, we were in the Swiss guardroom. They both saw me come in but continued talking, so I sat down in a chair and rubbed my feet.

Soon the guard went to a telephone on the wall and my friend came over and told me he was calling the American ambassador.

"*Signor*, this is dangerous business," I said. He smiled and said nothing.

Within a very few minutes a small man in a business suit came, followed by a priest.

"I am the secretary to the British Embassy, and this is Monsignor McGough," the little man said. "I understand you are an American."

"Yes, sir," I said.

"How did you get here?" asked the secretary, and then I related in detail the story of my being shot down and my walk through Italy. I gave him my identification card and other cards and things that I carried in my pocketbook.

Both men studied the cards very thoroughly, saying nothing for a time. I began to wonder what would happen next.

"How long ago did you say you escaped?" the secretary asked.

"It was the twenty-eighth of September last year," I answered.

The secretary handed me back my pocketbook and he and the Monsignor went into a huddle in the corner. Shortly, the Monsignor left through the door in the rear of the guardroom, and the secretary approached me.

"In a few seconds," he said, "you will see the Monsignor pass by the door," pointing to the door that I had just entered. "Follow behind him and he will take you to a safe place."

I thanked him, as well as my friend who had helped me, and when I saw the Monsignor pass by the door I waited a few seconds, then walked out of the door into the square.

The Monsignor was about a hundred yards ahead, and I decided that was about the proper distance. No one could observe any connection between the two of us. I would stop now and then to glance into a shop window and then continue on, at no time allowing myself to pay any noticeable attention to the person I was following.

We were on the outside of the great wall around the Vatican, and were following it to the right. I began to wonder where we were going. I was so sick I could hardly keep moving, but I couldn't give up and stop to rest.

We had walked a good mile when we came to another gate in the great wall. Two Swiss guards were walking back and forth as the Monsignor approached. The guards came together just as the Monsignor reached the entrance and they saluted as he nodded and passed into Vatican City.

The sweat popped out on my face, and I thought my knees would buckle under me. The guards had not moved since the Monsignor had passed through, but were still standing at attention facing each other. I had not slowed my pace and was within two hundred feet of them now.

The guards in their traditional striped uniforms and ancient helmets were holding fast, their long spears resting in a vertical position on the pavement.

I slipped my hand into my coat pocket and felt my automatic, but then I decided not to try to force my way in at gun point. I took my hand out of my pocket and kept walking.

Just as I approached the entrance, both guards did an about-face and started marching in opposite directions. I walked into Vatican City.

I was inside Vatican City, shaking hands with others who had successfully escaped into this famous free city. These boys took me in like a long-lost brother; and, believe me, I needed a brother or two about that time!

Regardless of the number of attempts I make, there just aren't enough words in the English language to describe the feeling that came over me. To me, this place was heaven, after walking endless miles in the heat of the Lombardian plain during the previous fall; stumbling over the snow-covered mountains of central Italy with nothing but a dim ray of hope that I might ever see our troops again; sleeping in stables, haylofts, and, occasionally, out in the open with an automatic pistol always cocked and ready; arousing suddenly at the slightest noise; listening breathlessly for footsteps meaning death or torture; awakening at dawn, still wet and cold, to start another endless journey; sweating out the German ambush, trapped like a rat and unable to move; and, through it all, waiting and praying that somehow I could be one lucky soldier that the Jerries would overlook.

The memories of begging some poor family to give me a worn-out pair of shoes in exchange for my pair with no soles so that I could keep going; seeing the look of despair on the children's faces around the table as I devoured a share of food that they should be getting; seeing the fear of death in the eyes of the parents, should I be caught in their home; being able to give each family in return for their hospitality only a note that Radio London screamed would be honored with food and help when the Allies arrived, yet realizing too well the futility of it all; sensing the joy of seeing my plans work or feeling the ever-increasing agony of a plan that failed—yes, these memories are, to an escaped prisoner, the real meaning of war—memories that will remain in my heart long after the world has forgotten.

As I lay in my bed that first day in the Vatican, I wondered. Was it sheer courage that kept me going all those months, or was I just a damn fool? It would have been easier to stay a German prisoner—I knew that. The Jerries had treated me well, and I didn't escape because of fear of ill treatment. I had lived in a free country twenty-three years, and no one had pointed a gun at me there and said, "You do this and that or else!" No one at home had made me hold up my hand and cry, "*Heil Hitler.*" None of my teachers in school had ever taught me to hate, deceive, and kill!

It was taking me all this time to figure out why I had escaped—guess I never had time to think about it before. I didn't like the idea of being behind barbed wire or being at the mercy of some damned arrogant German. All my life I had heard about the Americans fighting for freedom; and here I had been doing it all these months—more out of instinct than anything else. . . .

. . . This was Easter 1944. For the next few weeks, Winton Sexton lay seriously ill in the Vatican as a result of his incredible feat of endurance. He finally got his freedom when the American troops rolled into Rome at the beginning of June. He had certainly earned it.

10.

Escape in Korea

At the end of the Second World War, Korea, which had been occupied by the Japanese, was divided in two. The area north of the 38th parallel of latitude was administered by the Russians, that south of this line was administered by the Americans. As a result of this division, North Korea formed a Communist government and South Korea a Republican government aided by the United States.

In June, 1950, the people of North Korea invaded South Korea. The United Nations' Security Council called on all member nations to come to the aid of the South Koreans, and a small American force was at once sent there. Within a few months the reinforced United Nations Forces had not only pushed the North Koreans out of the south but had themselves occupied North Korea almost to its northern border with Manchuria (part of Communist China).

Now the Chinese Communists joined in, and by April, 1951, they had driven the United Nations Forces almost out of North Korea. In this month the Gloucestershire Regiment earned its nickname "the Glorious Glosters" by making a gallant stand on a hill near the Imjin River. In this battle, Captain Anthony Farrar-Hockley was captured by the Chinese Communists; for his gallantry in the action he was later awarded the Distinguished

Service Order (he already had the Military Cross for gallantry in action in the Second World War).

Farrar-Hockley's first attempt to escape was during a river crossing, when he lowered himself into the water and allowed the current to sweep him away from the column. For several hours he drifted with the current, getting clean away from his guards. He was recaptured while making his way through enemy lines.

He escaped for a second and a third time and each time had bad luck. The difficulty was not in getting away but in avoiding recapture in a land where his fair hair and blue eyes stamped him immediately as an enemy.

After his third attempt, Anthony Farrar-Hockley was incarcerated in a hole dug in the side of a hill, its entrance closed by an oil drum. He bored a tunnel through the earth from the back of his cave—and was free again. This time he reached the shore of the Yellow Sea before he was recaptured.

He was given a spell in a political prison before being taken to the combined working camp and interrogation center where this story opens....

... We made the final decision to escape while working on the hill one morning. After telling the story of my captivity to my new companions, very naturally the subject of another escape had arisen. With the rapid onset of the Korean winter, I had originally decided, after my discharge from Sinuiju jail, that I would take up winter quarters in a prison camp and make a fresh escape in the following spring. In any case I had Tom with me; and I had felt that I could not leave him alone with the North Koreans, knowing that he would suffer at least in part for my misdemeanor if I managed to get away. Now, talking to the two working with me—Jack, the young American flier, and Ron, the Australian —it seemed to me that circumstances had changed considerably from those on which I had based my former appreciation.

The first change had been that we found ourselves in a North Korean interrogation center, and not in a prisoner-of-war camp. Though we had not expected to find any luxuries in the latter, we had anticipated sufficient food to maintain life throughout the winter. Here we were getting a diminishing ration of boiled millet daily with a very thin soup, containing a bean or a radish leaf to convince our stomachs of its authentic nourishment value. Worse, Tom, who was under intensive interrogation, was being punished for his lack of response by being starved. His rations had been cut off completely, and they were now threatening to cut off his water supply. Our efforts to feed him from our own meager issue of millet had been circumvented; at mealtimes we were supervised to the point where the guard commander or a sentry actually watched us eat.

In the second place, the barn in which we were quartered was now bitterly cold at night. The North Korean troops in the village had all been issued with warm winter garments, but the interrogators made it clear that they would not issue clothing to those who did not cooperate with them. We were not cooperating and had no intention of doing so. It seemed as if the bitterest phase of the North Korean winter would find us in what threadbare garments we still possessed. Jack was the worst off. He had been shot down in midsummer, wearing only thin underclothing and a summer flying suit. Ron, who had parachuted from a Meteor shot down over Sinuiju, was only better equipped to the extent of a woolen shirt.

The staff of the interrogation center were the most unpleasant and unscrupulous captors I had encountered up to that time, being either fanatical Communists, sadists, or a combination of both. The commander was a lieutenant colonel of the infantry who spoke a little English. After our arrival, he had pointed out that, as war criminals of the worst sort, we could not expect a proper ration of food while awaiting our turn to be interrogated, unless we worked for it. This meant, in fact, hard labor, constructing air-raid shelters for his headquarters, digging and removing earth and rocks, carrying water for cementing over a long distance, and carrying timber and bricks up to the hill from the village. We were all weak from the privations of our captivity, and on our coarse, poor diet we were expending strength we could

Escape in Korea

ill afford. There were sometimes additional tasks in the evening. For instance, the officer who dealt principally with us was an infantry major—referred to by Kim, the civilian interpreter, as the Young Major. He hated us bitterly. Whenever possible, he would find us unpleasant tasks, such as cleaning out the filthy headquarters latrine—a huge stone jar sunk in the earth, which had to be emptied with a small can by hand into a leaking bucket. What enhanced his pleasure in setting us this duty was that he could refuse us permission to wash afterward, so that we must return to our quarters filthy with latrine matter. On other occasions, we had to work the crude machine that cut fodder for the cattle, or clean up the animal stalls—jobs we minded less because we were sometimes able to steal a *diacon* (a cross between a turnip and a radish), which, though raw and unpalatable, filled our empty bellies for a short time. I protested to Kim on my first two initial interrogations about this treatment, without result. He excused himself by saying that it was no affair of his, but betrayed his feeling, by replying to my remarks about the Geneva Convention and its prisoner-of-war clauses, with a comment that the Convention was an instrument of bourgeois reaction which, anyway, was inapplicable to war criminals such as ourselves. Kim was a vain man, who posed as an ex-professor in political economy at Seoul University, but he let slip to Jack one day that he had really been an announcer of the Seoul Radio. He had a marked inferiority complex and, like the Young Major, was really a savage under a thin veneer of education.

These were the circumstances surrounding our captivity—with a prospect of deterioration. Before we met that morning to make our decision, however, one other important aspect had been considered: Tom's future as a lone captive in the hands of a group of men who hated him, as an American major of the regular service, perhaps more bitterly than the remainder of us. He was, to them, the epitome of all the power and abundance of life which they coveted so much, feared so much, and thus hated so profoundly. What had led me to consider leaving Tom at all was that our escape might make our captors afraid that the news of his treatment would become known to the outside world. If successful, we could actually institute such inquiries through Kaesong to ensure that he received the care a human being might expect. But both Tom and I knew that their fury on discovering our absence might be so unbridled that he would not survive it.

The night before we took the final decision, I rolled over onto my side and began to whisper in Tom's ear, putting to him the prospect as I saw it and the hope that escape held for us. Tom said,

"Of course you must go. As the senior officer here, I order you to disregard my safety, if you feel you have a chance of making it."

I reminded Tom that he would be absolutely at the mercy of the Young Major's temper—a temper we knew to be demoniac in character.

"You must go," said Tom, again.

Knowing him, I should not have expected any other answer. On the following morning we reviewed the position and made our decision: I would begin work that night.

Initially, my interrogations had been conducted by Kim alone. These had been of a entirely political nature, in order to sound me out as a possible convert to their cause—or, at least, a cooperator. They had a young soldier elsewhere in the village, who had ostensibly accepted their views and supplied them with a certain amount of information after a terrible sickness that had left him looking like a skeleton. We saw him twice and he begged us, in a voice that might have belonged to a very old man, to abandon resistance to our captors. To his knowledge, he said, one American who had resisted them had already been starved to death in the very building we now occupied. He was led away from us by U, his principal instructor, who urged him not to waste his time speaking to us.

On the very night that I was determined to begin work on breaking out, I was called out after darkness for an interrogation by the Young Major, a Captain Li, and a lieutenant I called Poker Face. Kim interpreted; the others spoke no English, except for Li, whose vocabulary was extremely limited. As I followed Kim along one of the village paths to a hut just below the air-raid shelter on the hill, I wondered whether this was to be another political interrogation, or a military interrogation in earnest. If the latter, what would they ask me? I knew that the greater number of their questions to Tom were concerned with information he could not possibly have given them, even if he had been prepared to do so; for they had demanded all the details of the top-secret codes used by the Far Eastern Air Force Headquarters —insisting that he must know these as a major flying with an operational squadron in Korea! The questions they asked me that night were even more fantastic. When I was brought before the Young Major, he asked me through Kim:

"Give us the organization, means of recruitment and training, method of dispatch, and system of communication of the British Intelligence Services throughout Europe and the Far East."

I was so amused to think that they believed me to be intimately in the confidence of the War Office that I smiled. Captain Li began to hit me about the head with a heavy wooden ruler. After an hour of threats, blows, and a warning to reconsider my attitude during the next day, I was taken back to the barn.

At that particular time, the sentry on duty outside the barn door was an unpleasant youth with pimples, whom we called "Hoju" because he used this term to Ron. We loathed him because he delighted in making our lives difficult. It was he who had caused the straw that we lay on to be removed; who had spied on us during meals and seen us hiding food to give to Tom; who prevented us from visiting the latrine. Whenever he was on duty, we were forced to talk in whispers, or he would get the guard commander to separate us in different corners, and insist that we neither lie down nor stand up, but sit up. At first, we had tried humoring, then ignoring, him; finally, we resisted every command for as long as we could. I was glad to see him standing there on sentry, for I knew that before long he would be relieved. Though the attention he paid us was not directly intended to prevent us from escaping—it was merely a means of demonstrating to himself his power over us—his attention on this night might lead to disaster. I waited in the darkness until the new sentry came on, and then began my work.

I planned to cut a hole in the outside wall of the barn. The lower half of the wall was of brick and too hard for my poor tools; but the top half was of wattles and mud, running up between stout timbers from brick to roof. While working outside, I had picked up an old screwdriver and a rusty table knife. With these tools and a Schick razor blade that I had secreted since the days at Munhari, I had to cut away the hard mud, bound with chopped straw, and to cut out the wattles on which the mud was mounted. The sentry was fifteen feet away, at the far, gable-end of the barn, by the main entrance to the courtyard. To enter the barn, if his suspicions were aroused, he would have to come into the courtyard—a matter of five paces—unlock the door, and switch on the light. If I kept a careful watch, I might have time to assume a sleeping pose, but after a certain point in my work, I would not be able to explain why there was the outline of a hole in the wall above us! Knowing that I should probably fail to cut my way through completely in one night, I decided to reach a point on the first night that might be explained, if noticed during the next day, by a fall of mud from the wall. Of course, I could not begin to cut the wattles but hoped to be able to look at the few I had exposed in daylight, so that I should be able to make a work plan for the following night.

The next morning, when the guard commander opened our door to bring in our bowls of millet, we all came near to heart failure. Looking at the wall, we saw that a large number of the wattles had been laid bare, and that the main area of mud removed was just about the size for a man to crawl through! It seemed that the great dark patch shrieked at the guard commander and sentries to be noticed.

The day passed in the normal way. When we returned from work, we at once asked Tom if anyone had taken an interest in the wall. Apparently, it had remained unnoticed. We ate our evening meal, and settled down for the night, ostensibly to sleep. Hoju was on guard immediately after dusk that night, so we knew he would not be on duty again for six hours. Shortly after he dismounted, I began work.

Tom, Ron, and Jack lay back under the mats, listening to the talk of some of the officers of the interrogation center, whose room was in the western half of the barn. Once I began to cut the wattles, we became absolutely committed to escaping that night, and I increased my speed as much as I dared. Every noise, however slight, seemed to echo through the room. I felt that, at any moment, there would be a cry of alarm from the officers next door, chairs would be thrown back, and doors opened, and a crowd of infuriated North Koreans unleashed upon us. Now and again the anxious voices of one of the others would reach me, asking for a progress report, and I would reassure them as best I could. I removed a complete section of wattles, after about two hours' work, and began to cut the hard mud away that lay beyond them. After about ten minutes, I made a disappointing discovery: there was another section of wattles between us and the outside. Though the room was very cold, the sweat ran from my forehead, face, and neck, as I cut, prised, pulled, and scraped as quickly as I could. Another hour passed before the second section was free. I pulled away the mud that remained on the far side, touched a smooth, flexible surface, pushed against it, and felt my hand slide through into the cold night air outside.

I returned to the floor, where the three were lying beneath their mats. Jack and Tom were talking in whispers. Ron had fallen asleep! Waking him, I went back to the hole and crawled through as quickly as I dared, dropping onto my hands on the far side. The wide ledge that ran along the outside wall was covered with empty bottles, buckets, tin cans, an automobile tire, and an old cast-iron wood stove. Standing on the ledge, I removed the bottles and the stove to one side to make way for Ron, who was the next to come out. His head appeared in the hole, his shoulders, his hips. Suddenly, he lost his balance. He fell forward, swept the ledge with his arms, and knocked the stove onto the track below. A loud crash rang through the village.

Nearby was an ox, lying in its stable. As Ron disappeared back through the hole in the wall, I ran across to the ox and lay down behind him, waiting for the reaction to the alarm. Several minutes passed, but no sound came above the heavy breathing of the sleeping ox. After ten minutes, I returned to the hole and called to Ron in a whisper. This time he managed to get right out of the hole before knocking a bottle off the ledge, but I caught it before it could fall. Jack followed. The three of us moved, as planned, to a stack of dried cornstalks about eighty yards from the barn. Here, Jack and Ron concealed themselves, while I returned to the courtyard. We had completed the breakout.

In a corner of the courtyard was a pile of old padded jackets and a pair of padded trousers. It was most desirable that we should have these, because of the lightness of Jack's and Ron's clothing— I was afraid that Jack, especially, might suffer from cold shock once we reached the coast. I crawled back into the courtyard through an opening in the wall, normally used to pass fodder through to the cattle shed. Laden with clothing, I returned the same way to the cornstalks.

Both Jack and Ron felt much better when they had donned their new clothing. I took the old black raincoat that Jack had discarded and we set off across the rice paddy on a course that led northwest to the mountains. Neither shots nor other sounds of alarm reached us as we crossed the main Chinam-po highway, and left the interrogation center behind a hill—free men once more.

By morning we had put twelve miles between us and our prison; Pyongyang, a broad stretch of the Taedong River, and the fertile Taedong valley lay below us in the morning sun. Our hilltop gave us ample cover in which to rest from the night march. We ate our raw *diacons*, taken from the fields far back, as we discussed the route to the coast.

North of Chinam-po we knew the seashore was covered with soft mud that often ran out for more than five miles, even at high water. But there were deep-water inlets northward, and the port of Chinam-po would be about twenty miles south of the point at which we expected to find the sea. Ron and Jack agreed with me that we should turn north on reaching the coast, and seek the deep-water inlets and the fishermen's craft that lay in them rather than risk the sentinels of Chinam-po. Once we got to the sea, we could only hope that wind and tide would not be against us. The problem of water for the journey was one that concerned me most; for I felt that, in our present condition, we would not be able to hand the boat effectively if we remained at sea for more than a week without water.

After a second careful reconnaissance, we descended from our hill at dusk, with a stream and valley to cross before we could climb a range on the far side that led to the sea. The brown-and-yellow leaves lay everywhere as we passed through the woods on the lower slopes. There had been plenty of chestnuts here, but the village boys had taken them all, leaving the spiky cases strewn beneath the trees. Reaching the rice paddy in the valley, we made a detour around the first village that lay on our course. Beyond, the stream flowed fast and deep between high banks of soft mud. I was hoping that we would find a crossing place higher up, for I was anxious that we should not get our clothes wet; the heavy night frost would certainly freeze them, and we could not count on a sunny day to dry them out before another night fell.

A young civilian came suddenly upon us from a tiny side path, glancing curiously at us as we passed. We continued across the valley without looking back until he was out of sight, when we quickly ran back along the track we had crossed, changed our direction, and took the small, disused footpath that led along the riverbank. As soon as we reached good cover, I led the way into the bushes to see if we were being followed. Sitting there on the cold earth, we could hear nothing but the river noise below us. Only after ten or fifteen minutes did we hear light footsteps. Looking through the branches, I saw the civilian we had passed earlier coming along the footpath, looking carefully about him as he went. He passed without seeing us and I watched him take a path that led to the main track running to our right. Half an hour went by; he did not return. I decided to go on.

We made another detour to avoid the next village, and were about to descend to the stream again when we were challenged. I heard the action of a rifle bolt close by, and, as the moon emerged at that moment from the clouds, saw a sentry about twenty-five yards away, his rifle covering us. Jack and Ron were behind me. It was foolish of us all to get recaptured; their chance of withdrawal was better than mine. Signaling to them to crawl away along a rice paddy bank near by, I walked slowly toward the sentry, speaking in a normal voice, hoping to distract his attention.

Attending to me, he did not spot the other two. He halted me firmly when I was about ten paces from him. Each of us stared at the other: he did not know what to make of me; I wondered how I could slip away from the weapon that covered me.

The guard turned out. I was led into the guardroom in a nearby village, which we had not observed in our daylight reconnaissance because it lay in a reentrant. By this time I had decided to attempt a bluff and, in the friendliest voice I could raise, I said, "*Tovarich!*" pointing delightedly at a colored picture of Stalin on the wall.

The soldiers looked at me in puzzlement for a few moments. They regarded my black raincoat and the Chinese Communist cap that Tom had given me for the escape; they indicated my beard and blue eyes to one another as they discussed me among themselves. One of them came forward and said a few words to me in what I believed to be elementary Russian, and I replied heartily in gibberish, ending as many of my words as possible with "ski," "shi," "ish," and "off." As their brown eyes grew friendlier, I began to indicate that I must be on my way, pointing to their watches as if asking the time. I really believed that I was going to get away with it; for they were smiling now and two men shook my hand. With luck, they might take me out onto the path and escort me to the edge of the village. I was about to light a cigarette offered to me when the door opened and a North

Korean police captain entered. He stepped toward me, speaking rapidly and apparently fluently in a language that was certainly neither Korean nor Chinese. After a few sentences I realized that the game was up: he was evidently a Russian interpreter. I took a good pull on the cigarette and said in English,

"I'm afraid there seems to have been some sort of mistake."

By the look on his face, I could see that he intended to rectify it. I left the guardroom with my arms bound tightly behind me.

I spent a very unpleasant night, being wakened every half hour or so by the guard, just to make sure that I had not slipped out of my clothes and crawled through a crack in the floorboards. Two or three hours after sunrise, the door of my cell in the local police station opened and I looked up to see the commander of the interrogation center standing above me.

"Ah," he said, greeting me with a friendly kick. "So it is you they have caught. I wondered which one it was."

I was removed from the cell, still bound, and taken into another village, where Kim and a lieutenant colonel of the police were waiting for me. As I approached, Kim looked up to say,

"You have been very foolish. You must be killed for this, I think." His face was twisted with rage.

The whole party of seven or eight who had come out to fetch me breakfasted in a house while I remained outside. Their meal over, I was brought in for a preliminary examination. In order to infuse the proper spirit into all concerned, the police lieutenant colonel cocked his pistol, brandished it in my face, and then began to hit me over the head with it. He had made sure that my hands and arms were securely bound before he began.

We had agreed on the tale to be told if any one or all of us were caught. First, we should insist that Tom knew nothing of our plans to escape; that we had cut through the wall and slipped out while he slept. In this way we hoped to save him any further retribution. Next, someone had to take the blame for devising and planning the escape, and, as the senior officer in the party, it was my duty to assume this responsibility. Finally, at all costs, we were determined to conceal from them that we had intended to seize a boat and escape by sea, as we were most anxious to avoid any special watch being kept on boats in the future.

This was the story I now told. I told it during the first examination in the village; and I told it again at the Central Police Headquarters in Pyongyang in the afternoon of the same day. By this time I was sitting in an office containing three colonels of police, who, to my surprise, seemed to have nothing better to do than question a wretched escaped prisoner-of-war. It may have been, of course, that the prospect of losing prisoners who would report the conditions of captivity to the outside world was sufficient to command their personal attention. Whatever the reason, my interview with them that afternoon imposed on them at least a measure of responsibility for what followed.

Before I was taken from the room, an incident occurred that was typical of their irrationality. The first colonel, seated at a desk, said,

"You say you tried to escape because we treated you badly, gave you no winter clothing, and so on"—this was part of our story. "Well, we had no food, clothing, or medical supplies to spare. The inhuman bombing by the American aggressors in violation of all the laws of decency has withheld supplies from us. You must not blame us; blame your own side."

No sooner had Kim translated this than the second colonel spoke. Without reference to the previous remarks, he completely contradicted them.

"We have plenty of supplies: the bombing of the American aggressors has had no effect on our war effort. But we only give these things to those who understand the truth and cooperate with us. If you cooperate, you will receive the same as any other person."

As if this contradiction were not enough, the third colonel apparently decided that yet another was necessary.

"You can never have such things from us. You are a war

criminal, and thus have no status except as a criminal. Only because of our goodness has your life been spared."

Having translated these three statements, Kim led me from the room. Perhaps the colonels wanted to argue out who should have spoken and what should have been said. I was taken to a square stone building near by where the Young Major settled down to question me himself. Poker Face (the lieutenant) and Kim were with us. I had a feeling that the interview would not be a pleasant one.

Now, although we had agreed to tell a set story and I had told this, I had refused to say in what direction Jack and Ron continued when I was recaptured. At first, I considered giving them a false scent, but realized there was really no point in this. I was not going to give them the information, and I might as well say so. At each examination I pointed out that I was a British officer and could hardly be expected to provide them with details that would assist them to recapture my comrades. The Young Major now informed me that it was his intention that I should do so. An argument that lasted for about half an hour began. At the end, Kim was given instructions by the Young Major, which he translated to me.

"You think you can trick us with your lies; but you will never be able to do so. We are armed with the knowledge of scientific Marxist Socialism and can scientifically analyze your words. Furthermore, your attitude reveals your insincerity. You refuse to cooperate with us, and show yourself to be our bitter enemy. The Young Major now gives you your last opportunity to redeem your crime of making an escape and of forcing the others to do so by using the rank you held in the forces of the aggressor. If you do not take it, we shall have to adopt severe measures."

When he had finished, they all looked at me. I said, "I have told you how things stand. I have nothing more to say."

When Kim had translated this back to the Young Major, the latter rose to his feet and said what I believed to be the only English word he knew:

"Okay," he said, making for the door. "Okay."

His drawn pistol covering me, Poker Face intimated that I should follow, and, with Kim, we left the room.

The Young Major had set off down a passage. Almost at the end of this, on the left-hand side, was a steel door that had two handles on it of the lever type—levers six or more inches long, whose inner ends locked into recesses in the door lintels. As we passed through this door, I saw that it was very thick and that the greater portion between the two steel faces appeared to be packed with fabric of some sort. Poker Face closed the door, locking it with the two inside levers, and moved around to join the Young Major.

"Strip to the waist," said Kim.

My mind could not conceive the truth that my senses offered. We were all standing in a small square room, with cement-faced walls and a concrete floor. High above us, from a wooden ceiling, ropes trailed from metal rings. There were two more such rings in the left-hand wall. Under the right wall was a large barrel of water. One little chair, such as a child might use in kindergarten, was beside it; across its back lay more ropes, in a tangle. In the light of a single bright electric lamp that burned in the ceiling, I saw that there were stains on the floor and walls that looked very much like blood. As I stripped off my filthy, lousy shirt and sweater, I knew that I was in a torture chamber.

Yet my mind could not conceive it. I was living in the twentieth century—the year A.D. nineteen hundred and fifty-one. Surely these three men could never bring themselves to torture me in cold blood. Looking around at their faces, I saw neither passion nor compassion in any one of them. I threw my clothes to the floor, and Kim kicked them into the corner as Poker Face tied my wrists again. The Young Major spoke to Kim, who said:

"Kneel down."

Kneeling there, looking up at them, still unable to comprehend that this was really happening to me, I saw the Young Major's hand come around to strike me on the temple, as the first of a series of blows that he and Poker Face released upon me. Kim joined them when they began to kick; and it was he who covered my face when the Young Major saw that I was anticipating and ducking some of the blows. Just before the cloth came down over my eyes, I saw to my horror that the Young Major's face had assumed an expression of savage pleasure: he was really enjoying my suffering.

In my innocence, I had thought this maltreatment was to be either my punishment or a means of inducing me to give information about Jack and Ron. I discovered that it was merely the overture. The covering was removed and I was assisted by Kim and Poker Face into the tiny chair. I almost thanked them for what seemd to be an act of remorse or compassion. It was neither. They now bound my legs to the front of the chair, my arms to the two uprights at the back. My wrists, still secured, were tied down with a second piece of rope to the crosspiece between the two back legs. The Young Major kicked me in the chest and the chair fell over, with me, onto its back.

Poker Face now produced a towel, as the Young Major threw two or three dippers of ice-cold water over my face and neck, drawn from the barrel in the corner. Still I did not understand, thinking, as I lay shivering with the cold, that I was to be chilled to the bone by repeated dousing. But Poker Face placed the towel over my face and, a second later, more water was thrown over me. When I tried to rise—a pitiful attempt in which I just managed to lift my head forward a little—the Young Major put his boot on my mouth and shoved my head back again. More water struck the towel, some running off onto my bare chest— but some was absorbed. I tried to blow out some of the water that had seeped through into my nostrils and mouth. If they are not careful, I thought, they're going to choke me. And then, instantly, comprehension followed. That was exactly what they intended to do. I think I have never been so frightened in my life.

It was such a simple but effective torture. The towel completely covered my face, its ends resting on my chest below and on my hair above. The application of water provided just sufficient moisture to make the towel cling lightly to my flesh, and so hold it in place. Thus, every breath I drew was drawn through the toweling, the process of inhaling only serving to draw the material more tightly onto my face. While the towel was reasonably dry, I could breathe adequately. But as its water content increased toward saturation point, each successive breath provided less and less oxygen for my laboring lungs. My mouth and nostrils began to fill with water. I realized that I was dying as I shook my head from side to side in a last despairing effort to throw off the clinging towel mask. Poker Face or Kim took my head between their hands and held it steady as the Young Major poured on more water. I suffered another short, terrible struggle to breathe before sinking into a delicious, shadow-filled tranquillity.

Of course, I had thought they meant to kill me. The violence of their treatment had been such that I had not hoped to live when I understood their purpose. But they were more experienced than I.

The Young Major must have known exactly when to stop—perhaps the moment I became unconscious. I came to, still lashed to the little chair but now upright, the water pouring from my nose and mouth down my chest. I had come around rather quickly because the Young Major was applying the end of a lighted cigarette to my back at frequent intervals. I saw that he was smiling. It was not a pleasant smile. He was good enough to desist when Kim began to ask me for the information they wanted. About ten minutes later, the process began all over again: I experienced the same terror; my expectation of death was the same as before, yet concerned me less than the agony of finding my breath dying in my lungs. When, eventually, I was dragged from the room, they had tortured me in this way three times.

Scarcely able to walk, I left the building between two police officers who had been called in. They took me through the cold, overcast night to a concrete cell block about two hundred yards away, and handed me over to the warrant officer who was on duty. The cells were constructed on much the same lines as those at Sinuiju; the prisoners were sitting inside in the same way. The only difference I perceived then or later was that this appeared to be more modern and more strongly constructed. Two warders took me down the long passage that led past the cells, opened a door at the end, and guided me along an extension by the light of a flashlight. Finally, almost at the end of the passage, we came to an unlighted cell. A push sent me to the floor, where my legs were bound and the knots on my wrists strengthened. Satisfied that I was securely roped, the warders departed. The metal rang as the door closed behind them and the key turned in the padlock. Their footsteps echoed as they withdrew along the passage. The door to the main passage closed; the last vestige of light disappeared. For the time being, my tormentors were content to leave me, if not in peace, at least alone.

That was the first day. They came for me on the second day, but not on the third; again on the fourth day; again on the sixth. In between times, I lay on the concrete floor, taking refuge in a corner from the water than covered most of the cell. Each morning I was brought a bowl of boiled corn, but had no water to drink. So that I could eat, my wrists were released, but not my sore, throbbing ankles. Though I asked to go to a latrine, I was not allowed to do so. As I had contracted enteritis from either the *diacons* or the corn, my clothes were soon fouled; but the lice did not seem to mind. Day and night, as I lay there, they wriggled across my flesh, setting up considerable irritation wherever they feasted on my blood. Sometimes it seemed to me that my whole body was alive with millions of them, eating my flesh away. It was impossible to remain in one position for more than a few minutes at a time: the discomfort became almost unbearable; my joints seemed to be on fire. There was no light during those six days, except when I was led out to the torture chamber, or when my food was brought in. I lay forever listening for the sound of footsteps that would take me back to the little room with the water barrel in the corner.

When they brought me back on the evening of the sixth day,

my spirits were lower than they had ever been before. I could not disguise from myself that my resistance was weakening. Now I was reduced to the state where I said that I would endure it for one more time; and when that time came, for one more time again. I experienced that night periods of light-headedness, due, I think, to the severe beatings. Periodically I began to hear voices in my ears, and have vivid dreams of being with my family again. That day Kim had said to me,

"If we do not find them, I think you will be tortured to death. We have many ways of killing you slowly."

Sometime on the seventh day I realized that I had taken almost all that my mind and body could take. I prayed very hard; and I think my faith in God was never stronger. Within an hour my circumstances improved.

The door to the main passage opened and I saw a flashlight coming toward the cell. Another was switched on as three men reached my doorway. For a moment I thought that I was to be taken out again: Captain Li from the Interrogation Center came into the cell and stood over me, calling my name.

"You are very lucky," he said. "Tomorrow you will be shot."

Such was my condition that I was glad—grateful that I was going to die a clean death that was in keeping with my profession, instead of dying vilely, in fear and agony in the torture chamber, with my own cries in my ears. I confess I am not of that breed of men who manage to remain silent under torture: I swore and shouted at the inquisitors each time, as long as I had breath.

Captain Li departed, but not the other two. I saw that a Korean police officer stood outside with one of the warders, watching me turning over and over restlessly, seeking for ease that was never there. He spoke to the warder, who entered the cell and, bending over me, unfastened my wrists and ankles; then departed, relocking the cell door. Unsteadily, unused to this freedom of movement, I stood up. Two of my ribs were cracked from kicks; my head, shoulders, and thighs were sore and bruised; my back was covered with cigarette burns, which smarted at the slightest touch from my filthy clothes—but I was free to move again! If I wanted to move a leg, I could move it! I could raise my arms and lower them at will! For several minutes I experimented happily under the eye of the watching policeman, though I had forgotten him. He called me over to the barred window, where we stood face to face. He was a man of middle height, clad in the uniform of a captain of the police. In the torchlight, I saw that he wore spectacles.

"*Tambay, eso?*" he asked, after a moment. I shook my head; he knew I had no tobacco. He drew three cigarettes from his pocket and passed them through the bars and found some matches to give me. As I stood in front of him, smoking my first cigarette for many weeks, he shook his head, smiling at me with obvious sympathy.

After all that had happened, this simple act of compassion was too much for my self-control. The tears rolled down my bearded cheeks as we stood, in silence, regarding one another.

When Captain Li came into my cell on the following morning, my mind was at rest. The preceding hours had been passed comparatively comfortably, on a piece of matting that had been brought to the cell by another prisoner—apparently permitted some measure of freedom in return for doing chores for the warders. He was a Korean national of Chinese parentage who had spent some years at a high school in Harbin. His English was quite good, and we had a whispered chat. It seemed that I was in the political block of the jail—a bad block to be in, because its inmates were made to work longer hours than the ordinary criminals. Would the Americans rescue me? I said that I feared they had other commitments of a higher priority. He brought me some old rags, and with these I endeavored to clean some of the filth from my body. I scrapped my underclothing, feeling that I should not be requiring it very much longer. My greatest regret was that I had neither cap nor comb, so that I should appear rather an unkempt soldier before the firing squad. As a great luxury, I sat down on my little rice-straw mat in the corner, leaning my elbows on my knees.

I now had a little light, which, however faint, made a great improvement to the cell; for, shortly after being unbound on the previous day, some covering on the roof had been removed, revealing a small shaft about the diameter of a penny. Gradually, my eyes took full advantage of it. Sitting in the corner, I went over my life, realizing how lucky I had been to have had so much happiness. I felt sure that I had had far more in my years than any other occupant of the block. I hoped my family would be informed of my death without too much delay, so that there would not be prolonged anxiety.

When Captain Li appeared, I rose, picking up Jack's black raincoat, which had been thrown into the cell on the previous day. I thought it would cover my ragged clothes.

"Where you are going," said Captain Li, "you will not need that."

He was probably right. I let it drop back onto the mat and preceded him through the door. We marched back down the passage, emerging into a fine November morning. The sun was shining from a blue sky; the wind was light; the air was keen but not too cold now that the sun was up. Beyond the doorway, standing at ease on a mud square, I saw a file of soldiers armed with rifles. I wondered how far I should march with this firing squad before we reached the place of execution.

Captain Li said, "Go on," motioning toward the soldiers with his pistol. Saying the Twenty-third Psalm over to myself, I walked over to them, and was marched to the road that ran toward the center of Pyongyang. At that moment I was astonished to see Jack coming out of a nearby building.

"Do not talk," said Captain Li. Three soldiers with him separated us on either side of the road, before we could exchange more than a greeting. I was just wondering whether Jack was to be shot, too, and if so, who would be shot first, when everyone with us except Captain Li and the three men walking with him wheeled to the right and disappeared. We continued to walk along the sunlit road without a word, heading for the wooded hill

Escape in Korea

that stands in the center of Pyongyang City, overlooking the airfield across the river.

It was when we were crossing an open space of rice paddy between one suburb and another that an opportunity occurred to talk. Captain Li saw a friend whom he ran after, calling on him to stop. They began an animated conversation some distance away. The guards drew together in a group to light cigarettes and have a chat. Jack and I worked along the paddy bund toward one another and sat down.

"Where are we going?" asked Jack.

"I don't know," I replied. "Are you going to be shot?"

Obviously, he had not thought of this. "Can't say," he said, after thinking it over. As the guards continued to disregard us, we decided to settle a few more points. Jack told me that he had been caught with Ron two days before. After a short wait with their captors, they had been taken back to the Interrogation Center, where they had spent a miserable time. Both he and Ron had been badly beaten up, in spite of "confessing" to our story. In addition, Jack had been made to kneel for hours with a heavy board held up by his arms behind his back, receiving a rain of blows every time he moved. Tom was recovering from several heavy beatings. Apparently six of them had considered it safe to attack a one-legged man after removing his crutches, while two men had covered him with pistols, in case he leaped to his foot and overcame them. He was still very weak from this and through his former starvation—concluded two days ago—and from a fever, given him by being drenched with cold water and left in a bitter wind. Both he and Ron had been taken off that morning in a jeep with the Young Major to an unknown destination. Kim had remained at the farm, while Li had brought Jack on foot to the Central Police Station. He was just telling me that he and Ron had turned south at the coast instead of north, when Captain Li returned. To my surprise, he did not seem annoyed that Jack was near me and obviously conversing. Instead, he made a remark that sent my hopes soaring to the blue sky.

"You understand," he said, tapping his pistol and looking at me very directly, "if you try to escape again, I shall shoot you."

We had a long, hot march—the more fatiguing because we were both weak and had had no food that day. Southeast of the city we came to a small coal-mining town where we met a jeep at the main crossroads. My spirits were not so high when I saw that the Young Major was sitting in it.

He was very affable, nodding and smiling at us; but we did not return his courtesy. After a few minutes' conversation, he got out and entered a restaurant, leaving us to climb into the jeep with Captain Li. I was very pleased to leave the Young Major behind us and to continue the journey on wheels.

After some miles of open country, where we passed at intervals Chinese-manned flak batteries, presumably defending Pyongyang, we drew up at the entrance to a disused coal mine. Captain Li handed us over to North Korean soldiers at an office, and, suddenly becoming very friendly, he handed us all the cigarettes in his packet as he departed for Pyongyang.

"What do you make of that?" said Jack, as he disappeared. "Two nights back that bastard was beating the hell out of me!"

We marched across the principal mine road to another office on the far side of the hill, where our names were taken by two North Korean Army officers. Then we were escorted toward a group of huts near by. As we reached the doorway of the last hut, there was a great shout; welcoming words greeted us; on all sides friendly faces appeared: Henry, Spike, Mike, the South African, Ronnie our Gunner, Tom, Ron—and new friends, British, American, French. It was almost a second homecoming as we were borne inside....

... Although Anthony Farrar-Hockley continued undaunted in his attempts to escape, the odds were always against him and he was cheated of final success by the truce and the exchange of prisoners that followed it.

11.

Through the Iron Curtain

For many people in Europe the end of the Second World War was not the end of oppression and suffering. In Hungary, for instance, the victory of Russia over Germany meant the creation of a new Communist system of government, which is ruthless in its suppression of everyone who is not wholeheartedly in its favor. No opposition of any kind is allowed, and all non-Communists who are not able to hide their true beliefs from the Secret Police are killed, sent to concentration camps, or forced to flee the country.

It is not easy to escape. The borders between countries dominated by the Soviet Union and the rest of the world are the most heavily guarded in history, and form the barrier that Sir Winston Churchill christened the "Iron Curtain." Even the seashore of satellite countries is patrolled by armed soldiers night and day; all boats are guarded, and no civilian is allowed on the beaches from seven in the evening until seven the next morning. The whole system of government is based on terror and force.

Christine Arnothy was only fifteen years of age when the

Russians marched into Budapest, the capital of Hungary. For the next three years she hid with her family in the country. At last it became obvious that a free life would never be possible under Communism, and the family decided to escape through the Iron Curtain into Vienna.

For fear of being given away to the Secret Police by informers, the escapers could not carry any luggage; instead they wore as many of their clothes as possible and stuffed their pockets full with small possessions. . . .

. . . Every one of our movements had been minutely studied for weeks. We knew exactly what answers to give if anyone questioned us. First of all, we were to go to the station. We were only to take tickets to the next station so that the booking-office clerk could not tell anyone where we were going. At the next station my father would take tickets as far as the frontier town. If, on the train, a patrol came and asked us what we were going to do in Ovaros, we should talk about Aunt Charlotte, a distant relative who lived there and who had invited us to visit her. When we arrived at Ovaros, we should try to get off the train as inconspicuously as possible and go to the house of the man who slipped people over the frontier, in an outlying part of the town. He would escort us to the station of the first Austrian village on the other side. From there, we should proceed to Vienna. We had enough money to pay the guide and to buy two thousand Austrian schillings. After that, we would see what happened. Such was our plan. There was nothing to do at the moment except to take care that everything went according to plan. Otherwise we might completely lose control of events and of ourselves. . . .

We went slowly down the main road. It was only round about five o'clock, but it was already dark. It was raining. The dog bounded along in front of us. He would run on, then stop and retrace his steps to make certain he had not lost us. My father walked with difficulty; he did not see well in the dark. My mother held my arm. I was perspiring. My layers of garments stifled me.

Through the Iron Curtain

We arrived at the station.

In the distance the train was approaching with an ever-increasing din. At last it came into the station. We climbed up the steep iron steps to the compartment. The dog made despairing leaps to follow us and had managed to hoist himself up onto the lowest step when another passenger, an elderly man who was impatient to get in, brutally kicked him off. Not in the least discouraged, the dog jumped up again, but the doors were already shut. Standing in the corridor, I could not manage to get the window down; it was jammed, or too stiff. I pulled it with all my might and I felt one of the dresses I was wearing had split. Sweat was beginning to trickle down my back, and I could feel tears running down onto my chin. I leaned my face against the glass so that no one should notice I was crying, and, in despair, I fixed my eyes on the deserted dog, staring with blurred eyes through the misted pane.

The train was moving and the dog was barking; he began to run along the platform, beside the coach. His thin, ugly little paws carried him at breakneck speed and I had the impression that he was catching up to us, that he was going to leap onto the carriage step. But he grew smaller and smaller; already he had stopped barking, he had only enough strength left to run. And then he was no more than a little speck. The train had left the station and was steaming along between the dark fields.

I went into the compartment. Three people were installed in it besides my parents: two men and a woman. The silence was complete: you could hear nothing but the rattle of the wheels. Before the war, these coaches had been enlivend by the chatter of the passengers. Nowadays no one dared to enter into conversation. Any sentence might be dangerous, and it was impossible to know who might not be a police spy. This silent journey had something frightening about it. I hadn't brought a book with me. I shut my eyes and leaned my head against the back of the seat. The gaze of the woman sitting opposite me burned through my closed eyelids. I decided to gaze at her in turn; it was the only means of making her turn away her head.

The ticket collector appeared. He punched our tickets without saying a word.

"How many minutes do we stop at Belatelep?" inquired my father.

"We don't stop there at all," said the ticket collector, suddenly becoming more talkative. "It's two days now since they cut out that stop for the evening train."

The woman with the piercing eyes began to stare at us again, with interest. This time it was my mother who extricated us from our tricky situation. She said to my father,

"Then it would be better to go and see them on the way back from Ovaros and not to break our journey now. You could take tickets on to there, couldn't you?"

"Is it possible to extend our tickets as far as Ovaros?" inquired my father.

The ticket collector nodded his head and dug out of his pouch a block interleaved with sheets of carbon paper. How complicated it is to take one's ticket on the train! The ticket collector had to make inscriptions in three separate places, but, finally, everything was arranged and my father put the tickets in his pocket. We would have liked to take off our coats but did not dare to, for the others would see our heavily padded shapes. There was nothing, perforce, for us to do but to remain sitting in silence, motionless with suspense.

"I don't believe it's raining anymore," said my mother, after an endless lapse of time.

My father nodded, and let his cigar ash drop on his overcoat. He promptly brushed it off with scrupulous care. The train grew emptier and emptier the nearer we approached the frontier town. The disagreeable woman began to collect her things; so did the two men. It was only then that we realized they were traveling together. They had not spoken, any more than we had. At last we saw them get out.

My father consulted his watch.

"The train's on time," he affirmed.

We went out into the corridor. The train slowed down and ran into the station of Ovaros. We were the only people who got out. This was far from reassuring. It was half past nine. Having sweated in the train, we now found ourselves shivering in the wind and the moonlight. A platelayer was running along the track, a red lantern in his hand.

"If they ask us anything . . . Aunt Charlotte!" repeated my father, and, tickets in hand, we made our way to the exit. Finally, we found ourselves together again outside the station, in an almost deserted street. Two policemen were standing on the pavement opposite. They stared at us.

"Don't turn around," my father told me. "Let's walk faster."

We followed him. He knew his way. He had prepared our flight with the utmost care. We left the center of the town and went farther and farther away from it through a maze of little, narrow, sparsely lighted streets. When we reached the outskirts my father knocked on the door of a house with dark windows. The door opened almost at once and a warm, unpleasant smell assailed our nostrils. A woman ushered us in and led us into a room lighted by a blinding, high-powered bulb. The curtains were meticulously drawn. I gave a hasty glance around. On a cooking stove, which gave out an infernal heat, a saucepan exhaled a thick steam reeking of onions. A fat man was sitting at a table, busy eating. He did not even get up when we came in, but merely signed to us to sit down.

"It's off for tonight!" he said, between two spoonfuls. His chin was fleshy and I should like to have seen his eyes, but he kept them greedily fixed on his soup.

"But why?" asked my father, in consternation.

The man at last decided to look at us.

"Because of the moon, of course. Shines too much. Lights up everything. Can't possibly set off like that. Anyway, I don't want to risk my skin."

The woman put another dish down on the table. I scrutinized the face of the guide. I had listened so intensely to his explanations that the meaning of the sentences escaped me. I only understood one thing: It's off. Perhaps tomorrow . . . It was nothing to do with him; *he* had no control over the moon. Then he gave us to understand that we must go away and come back at half past nine the next night.

"But where can we spend the night and the whole of tomorrow?" asked my father. "We can't go to a hotel—the police would be warned at once."

He waited for the guide to suggest our spending the night in his house. But the fleshy-chinned peasant was positive and peremptory; he had undertaken to make us cross the frontier, period. There was no question of staying in his house; the police made too many searches, and they'd been keeping their eye on him for some time. He would only make the trip once or twice again, not more. This kind of business was getting too dangerous.

His wife added in a toneless voice,

"You'd do better to go at once. Come back tomorrow night."

We definitely had to make up our minds. But where were we to go? I was hungry.

"Could you give me a little water?" I said, in the hopes of being offered something to eat.

With a brusque movement, the women ran some water into a thick-rimmed cup. She thrust it into my hands. I only took two mouthfuls of it. The water was warm and smelled of disinfectant.

A few moments later we found ourselves once more in the street. It was essential to start walking at once in a definite direction, as if we knew where we were going. Strollers were suspect, and if we were asked for explanations, all was lost. So we set off with a firm, decided step, like people afraid of arriving late at the place where they are expected.

"Where are we going?" I asked, panting.

The cold air I breathed in cut like a knife.

"There may still be one possible chance," said my father. "But if that does not succeed, there's no other solution for us but to take a train again and to travel until tomorrow evening. Impossible to go to a hotel, and the station waiting room is only too often raided by the police."

We traversed unknown streets and arrived at last in front of a church. My father went up the steps and we followed him. The heavy door was not locked. We pushed it open. In the dense shadow, the sanctuary lamp gave out a faint glimmer before the invisible altar. Utterly worn out, my mother, and I sat down in the last row of benches. As to my father, he disappeared. Were we to remain sitting here till daylight? And what were we to do for the whole of the rest of the day? We could not stay in a church for twenty-four hours. I ought to pray now, but I had not the strength to. I was cold, I was hungry, I was sleepy.

My father returned and touched us on the shoulder.

"Come," he whispered.

We followed him. We walked down the nave and went into the sacristy. It was completely dark in there. But a gleam that filtered through the crack of a door allowed us to see a priest who was standing in front of us. He shook hands with us and invited us to follow him. He told us in a low voice,

"Be very careful, I implore you, and crouch well down as you walk, the moment you get into the room we're going to. The window has no curtains and a street lamp shines in from the street. The house opposite is a police station, and the policemen can see everything that goes on inside. If we were to put up a curtain it would rouse their curiosity."

I wished I could see this priest's features so as to judge how much charity and how much fear there was in his makeup, but he had no face. He opened the door for us and went into the room, bending down as low as possible. The lamp in the street outside swayed in the wind and its shadow swung to and fro on the wall. We sat down on the floor.

"We can stay here till tomorrow evening," my father told us.

"However did you manage to arrange this?" asked my mother.

But the question remained unanswered.

"We must get undressed," said I.

"Only our coats," replied my father.

Never had I imagined it was so difficult to take off a coat while remaining squatting on the floor. We helped each other as best we could. My father was elderly and his blood pressure was high, but he made no complaint. Outside, the wind redoubled its violence. The street lamp shot its beam of light onto the opposite wall, sent it dancing up to the ceiling, where it disappeared in a flash; then, a moment later, the whole process began again. I was seized with giddiness, as if I were on a ship. I shut my eyes but the light hurt me, even through my eyelids. A strange sensation of seasickness came over me. My sweat-soaked clothes were stifling me and my sick uneasiness was dragging me down to the land of nightmares. I wanted to open my eyes, but the luminous pendulum, which kept swinging ever faster and wider, paralyzed me. Then, in the dizzy vortex of anguish and drowsiness, a mouth appeared to me: a mouth with curving lips. To whom could that mouth belong and where could I have noticed it so clearly as to be sure I had seen it before? The mouth smiled and spoke to me, but I could not hear the words it uttered.

The night of torture dragged on. One moment we were crossing the frontier, but the oscillations of the lamp brought me back to reality. It was two o'clock in the morning. My parents were asleep. To whom had that mouth belonged? Sleep overcame me once more. I was running along a dark road. A dead man came to meet me, one of those who had lain in front of our house in Budapest. He signed to me and smiled.

"They've stolen the wedding ring off my finger," he told me, gaily. "I'm going to reclaim it from the thief. No doubt he'll give me back my arm, too."

I noticed that he had lost an arm and that a flower was growing out of the wound and getting bigger every moment until it finally blotted out the dead man's face.

At last it was daylight. We recovered the dregs of our strength as a wounded man does on the battlefield when dawn revives him enough to drag himself along, crawling, toward the village.

Crawling like that, we left the room.

In the passage we stood upright and walked along to a narrow recess where we found what we needed to make a sketchy toilet. We still had to keep all our clothes on. Soon afterward we found ourselves squatting once more in the room where we had spent the night. An old priest, with an impassive face, brought us some coffee. He put the cups down on the floor as if that were the natural place to put them. He said nothing and behaved as if he scarcely noticed we were there. The time passed with atrocious slowness. Heaven grant there would be no moon tonight! So far, the weather was cold and rainy. The sky was muffled and gray.

We sat motionless for hours; then, once again, it was dark. The dance of the streetlamp started up once more. Six o'clock. After an interminable time of waiting, at last it was eight o'clock. I hid my face in my hands to shield my eyes from the light. I had the feeling that I was pressing my face against someone else's hand. This feeling was not new to me, but whose hand was it and when had it stroked my face before?

At nine o'clock we crept out of the room. The priest was standing there in the dusk and nodded us good-bye. We went through the sacristy, then once again we were in the church. The wan light of the sanctuary lamp made a faint red haze before my eyes. Then we were delivered up to the night. As we made our way, we kept anxiously scanning the sky. Thick clouds were heaped up so low that they looked close enough to touch.

The door of the guide's house opened at the first knock. This time the couple were more amiable. The wife was preparing some mulled wine for us.

"Wine? At this moment?" my father asked incredulously.

"I make everyone have some before we set off," said the guide with a grin. "Gives 'em strength and raises their morale. I can't undertake anything with people who are frightened. And everyone's frightened on an empty stomach, even me. So come on, let's drink."

He emptied a great mug of steaming wine. I raised mine to my lips and tasted this liquid. It was spiced and scalding hot. But my palate soon became accustomed to it and I emptied my mug avidly and resolutely. This drink warmed up our tired and famished bodies as if new blood had been injected into them. The room suddenly looked bigger to me and the guide's face rounder.

"I've drunk it all up," I said thickly, giving a broad grin.

I had the impression that my mouth was split to the ears and that I should never manage to be serious again.

"Well done!" said my father. His spirits had risen, too. Then, with an elegant, airy gesture, he indicated the door.

"Can we leave now?"

The guide took another draft.

"Too much," said my mother uneasily. "Too much. If you drink too much, you'll lose your way."

"And if he does lose it? What'll happen?" I said, with my mouth wide open as if for a guffaw. I wanted to cry, but I only laughed louder than ever.

The plump little peasant seemed suddenly to make up his mind.

"We'll be off," he said, putting on his leather coat. He kissed his wife and gave us some instructions.

"Never walk one beside the other. Always in file, as if we weren't together. If I stop, you stop. If I lie down flat, you do the same. If I run, you run."

My father interrupted good-naturedly,

"I'm sixty, my friend. It's not easy for me to run, you know."

The peasant turned suddenly icy.

"Anyone who's running to save his life hasn't got any age," he said, pulling in his belt. "On your way!"

We went out into the blackness. The guide in front, my mother next, then I. My father came last. We kept a distance of six or eight paces between us. It was a quarter to ten. The street was deserted. Our footsteps echoed as if we were walking under an arch. Soon we left the town and found ourselves in the vineyards. They were well tended. But how difficult it was to walk there! The earth was rough and slippery. It was very dark. The

guide went forward at a rapid pace and, at all costs, we had to follow him. My father stumbled and uttered a stifled cry. The guide growled,
"Silence."
My father was finding it difficult, walking in the dark; he kept slipping on the clods of earth. I longed to give him my arm but, among the vines, we could only advance in Indian file. At last, we arrived at the foot of a hill. A stream flowed in front of us and the rain had begun to fall again. It protected us, for it made visibility very poor. The frontier guards could see no better than we did.

The darkness was dissipating the effects of the alcohol. I stared at my feet and listened to the dragging sound of footsteps. I was past knowing whether I was frightened or not. The moment was something beyond my grasp; events were too overwhelming for me, and I felt as if I had been swept beyond the limits of human comprehension. I went on walking.

The guide stopped abruptly and, with a motion of his hand, gave us the order to squat down. Panting, we sat down in the wet grass. How good it was to sit down for a little! It was eleven on the luminous dial of my watch.

Was it possible we had already been walking for an hour and a half? The sweat began to chill again on my back. I was thirsty.

The guide came up to us without raising himself upright.

"I don't know if they've already gone past," he whispered. Then he added, "I'm frightened."

It was more irritating than alarming to hear him say he was frightened. What must we be feeling if *he* was afraid? We lay down in the soaking grass. Not far from us ran the main road. The asphalt showed pale and smooth in the darkness. It was nameless anguish to know that we would have to cross that broad, clear gap. How much longer would we have to stay here, waiting? The distant blast of a whistle rent the silence. Some instants later, a car went by. The shape of the guide reared up again.

"They've gone," he said. "We can try and get across."

"Is the road the frontier?" I asked him.

He stressed his impatience with a little shake of his head.

"Of course not. The frontier's still a long way."

Where was the frontier? What was the frontier like? We reached the edge of the road. The cemented surface spread before our eyes as if an invisible hand were widening it in front of us.

"Run!" ordered our guide.

My parents crossed the high road as if it were a skating rink. They wanted to run, but all they could do was stumble. We were in the middle. An inner force urged me to run, but I followed the pace of my parents. The guide had already been on the other side for a long time. He gesticulated and muttered oaths.

"At last!" he said, when we arrived. "Now there's a clearing—and then the forest begins."

The road stretched behind us like a silver ribbon. We ran through the clearing and finally reached the trees. I leaned against the first damp trunk and got my breath back, pressing my face against the bark.

The guide never stopped grumbling:

"This is the very last time I ever do this job with old people. It's impossible. They creep along like slugs."

We continued on our way, plunging into dead leaves up to our ankles. It was very dark. From time to time, a wet branch brushed against my face. And it was then that, suddenly, during that crazy journey, I realized to whom that nameless mouth and that caressing hand had belonged.

To Pista. I saw him again as I had seen him one day when he had said something to me, very close by the candle. I could not remember what he had said to me but I saw his mouth again and the gleam of his splendid white teeth. And the hand had belonged to him too, that hand that had helped me cross the plank above the drowned man. It was then that he had stroked my cheek. And I had only realized it at this moment. But, yes, at this very instant he was near me. He was holding my hand.

"Lie down," hissed the guide. "Lie down."

We were lying full length in the leaves, but now I no longer felt so abandoned. Pista was there to help me to surmount these last difficulties. The guide ordered us to go on. All I heard was his authoritative voice; all I felt was the contact of the wet soil; it was dark, I could see nothing. I could hardly hear the labored panting of the two tortured elderly people. We walked on. We walked fast, making an agonized effort and I did not feel strong enough even to glance at my watch.

The forest was growing less dense; the guide was becoming more and more uneasy and hostile.

"You'll have to pay more. For old ones like you, I shall ask extra."

"You shall have all you want, but get us across the frontier," said my father, and his voice reached me from very far away. Yet he was only a few steps from me.

We came to a clearing then; suddenly, the moon began to shine with all its brilliance, with all its celestial coldness. Our guide started swearing again. I no longer paid the least attention to him. Water was running all down my neck, my hair was soaked, and my damp clothes imprisoned me like a cuirass. The dazzling moonlight flooded the black landscape with white.

"That's the frontier," growled the guide. "And that infernal moon has to shine! We'll have to run. . . . Go on—run—even if it kills you!"

Why had I always believed that a frontier must, of necessity, be a material obstacle? A barrier—or a wall like the ones that border certain mountain roads? And now I saw, as I ran, stupefied, and sobbing with the effort, that the frontier was only black grass and moonlight. I walked in the light as if drenched in a bath of silver and there, where it shone most intensely, there where my hand and my hair and my heart were whitest—that was where the frontier lay.

I swathed myself in those enchanted rays.

Darkness suddenly asserted itself again, after the clearing. And I heard the voice of the guide, relaxed now,

"You can sit down; we're in no-man's-land."

I collapsed beside my parents. I pressed one cheek against the earth, against that earth which belonged to no one and which was mine. This was where I was at home: here, where spirits met again in the luminous void that stretched between the two parts of the world.

"Let's go on," said the man, after that brief repose.

We were treading on Austrian soil. But the station we had to reach was still a long way off. My mother took off her shoes and wrapped her feet up in her silk scarf, which she had just torn in two. She walked the rest of the way like that. My father lurched along, staggering, but his courage remained unshaken.

Dawn found us in a little Austrian station. Street vendors and men in short leather breeches occupied the waiting room. They spoke a language I did not understand. It was the first time in my life that I had been in a foreign country. If I had begun to speak, people would have looked at me with astonishment. Our guide withdrew in company with my father; when he returned, he held out his hand to us.

"You're in luck. For the present, you're safe. Your train to Vienna leaves in ten minutes."

And, having made this farewell, he disappeared into the crowd.

Here we were, alone together once more. My mother put on her shoes again. My one craving was an inexpressible longing to drink a cup of boiling-hot coffee.

"I bought two thousand Austrian schillings from him," explained my father. "He let me have them at a fair rate of exchange and he's taken tickets for us as far as Vienna. A thoroughly decent fellow! I only hope he gets back without any hitch."

I asked, "How long will these two thousand schillings last?"

My father considered.

"About two months. At least I hope so."

"And, after that, what will become of us?"

"After that, we shall have to begin our life all over again. . . ."

The waiting room was becoming more and more animated. The

women loaded themselves with their big baskets and bustled out onto the platform. We, whose limbs were quite benumbed, draggeed ourselves along like half-unconscious survivors of a shipwreck who struggle against the undertow and reach dry land with their last gasp.

Stiff with sleep, we managed to sit upright on the wooden benches of the little local train. A sullen ticket collector punched our tickets with complete indifference. Opposite me, a man lighted his pipe with ritual care. The nauseating smell of cheap tobacco turned my stomach. It began to rain again. The landscape melted into the gray sky. In the distance, factory chimneys went by, one after another. So did ruins, and still more ruins. I had the impression that I had been in this train for years, as if fate had nailed me to this hard wooden seat and forced me to travel unceasingly past endless ruins, in the company of silent beings. I had believed that, beyond the frontier, beyond Hungary, in the countries they called Occidental, the sky would be blue and the people happy. I had thought they would surround us joyfully and that their smile of welcome would make us forget the past. But, in this train, nobody smiled at all and the tobacco smoke became thicker and thicker and more and more unbearable.

We were getting near Vienna. I looked avidly out of the window. My heart beat fast. How many times my parents had talked to me of that enchanted city, always sparkling with gaiety. The train stopped in the midst of ruins. This must be the station, since everyone was getting out. We, too, got out. The rain trickled down the charred walls and dripped off the broken gutters. In a few seconds we were soaked to the skin. The crowd swept us along with it toward the exit. My coat was getting heavier and heavier, and I would like to have split through that cocoon of wretched clothes I had worn for three days without being able to take them off. Suddenly I felt the fastenings that kept up my nightdress giving way. Impossible to stop it from unrolling its full length! There I stood, with the rain running down my face onto my gray coat, whose hem showed several inches of silk nightdress. I felt impotent and ridiculous. That light blue contrasted so sharply with the dingy gray that it was beginning to attract stares. People stopped and looked at me without the faintest smile. I rushed forward, in tears, toward a nearby hut. The nightdress hindered my running, clinging to my ankles; the muddy water soaked through my shoes and splashed my clothes. When, at last, I got under cover, I had to wait till my hands stopped trembling. At first I wanted to tear the silk that had come down at such an awkward moment, but the material resisted. It was stronger than I was. There was no other solution but to pin it up. At last I was able to rejoin my parents and we left the station. The curtain of rain blocked our view. Where, oh where, was Vienna?

We set off walking at random. Chance brought us to the door of a café. We went into it. The waiter gave one glance at us, then resumed his chat with a customer. At another table, a couple was drinking coffee. The man occasionally spoke a few words; the woman never answered.

We sat down. The waiter came up and flicked a duster over the table.

"Three coffees and something to eat," my father said in German.

We were so utterly exhausted that we could find nothing to say to each other. We sat, motionless, looking out into the street where the wind was now making the rain swirl. A stout old lady pushed open the door and entered, carrying a very fat dachshund in her arms. That reminded me of our own dog. Perhaps he was still running—despairingly in pursuit of the train and of his faith in human beings.

The waiter brought the coffee and three minute gray rolls. I bent my head over the cup and closed my eyes. I drank. The beverage was only coffee in name, but it was scalding hot and it warmed both body and heart. Already, the street seemed to me less hostile. I devoured one of the little rolls. At that moment, I caught sight of myself in a mirror opposite me and I noticed that I was smiling. . . .

3 9123 00121232 8
HACKENSACK-JOHNSON LIBRARY

a3912300121232 8b

J904   281341
Williams
The will to be free.

89

DATE DUE

Johnson Free Public Library
Hackensack, New Jersey